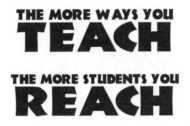

THE MORE WAYS YOU
TEACH

THE MORE STUDENTS YOU
REACH

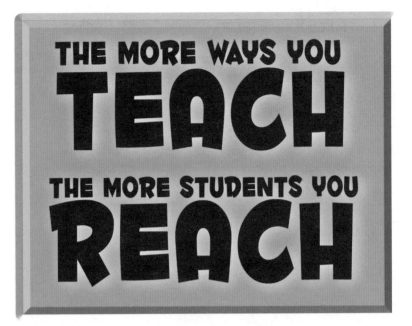

THE MORE WAYS YOU TEACH THE MORE STUDENTS YOU REACH

86 Strategies for Differentiating Instruction

Char Forsten, Gretchen Goodman, Jim Grant, Betty Hollas, and Donna Whyte

Crystal Springs BOOKS

A division of SDE Staff Development for EDUCATORS

Peterborough, New Hampshire

Published by Crystal Springs Books
A division of Staff Development for Educators (SDE)
10 Sharon Road, PO Box 500
Peterborough, NH 03458
1-800-321-0401
www.crystalsprings.com
www.sde.com

© 2006 Crystal Springs Books
Illustrations © 2006 Crystal Springs Books

Published 2006
Printed in the United States of America
10 09 08 07 06   1 2 3 4 5

ISBN-13: 978-1-884548-93-2
ISBN-10: 1-884548-93-8

Library of Congress Cataloging-in-Publication Data

The more ways you teach the more students you reach : 86 strategies for differentiating instruction / by
    Char Forsten .. [et al.].

    p. cm.

  Includes bibliographical references and index.

  ISBN-13: 978-1-884548-93-2

  ISBN-10: 1-884548-93-8

1. Teaching. 2. Effective teaching. 3. Individualized instruction. I. Forsten, Char, 1948- II. Title.

LB1025.3.M666 2006

371.102--dc22

                        2006018840

Editor: Sandra J. Taylor
Art Director, Designer, and Production Coordinator: Soosen Dunholter
Illustrator: Joyce Designs

Contents

. . . .

COMMUNITY BUILDING

ASSESSMENT

MANAGEMENT

TEACHING TOOLS

Introduction

Open any newspaper, magazine, or journal these days and you will likely find front-page articles about children and education. There are reports on the effects that poverty can have on children and how they learn; statistics on the growing population of students from diverse cultural backgrounds whose primary language is not English; and most recently, studies showing that boys, who are biologically, developmentally, and psychologically different from girls, are falling behind and are twice as likely as girls to be diagnosed with learning disabilities and to be placed in special-education classes.

At the same time, there is a growing body of evidence, from research-based data to classroom success stories, indicating that differentiated instruction is the answer to these diverse and ongoing challenges. So why would anyone hesitate to put differentiated instruction into practice? Perhaps the thought of redoing a familiar and comfortable lesson plan makes you uneasy. Or, the idea of managing multiple groups of students or individuals seems overwhelming, if not impossible. Or, simply, the notion of devising new ways for delivering information sounds absolutely exhausting. But don't despair—there _is_ good news.

Based on our experiences and successes using differentiated instruction, we have compiled our best practices in this book, making sure that the strategies cover a variety of categories (literacy, math, community building, assessment, management, and teaching tools) and learning modalities (visual, auditory, kinesthetic, and tactile). To make differentiating instruction as accessible as possible, we have included strategies that can be easily modified to fit various parts of the curriculum. In addition, we've provided ways to make them more or less complex so that you can teach and reach all of your students—from those who have learning difficulties to those who are gifted, and those who are in between.

The primary intent of differentiated instruction is to maximize student capacity, to find different pathways for students to learn and practice skills and concepts. For example, some students may understand the concept of division but have difficulty with number sense or math facts. The activity on page 48, "Divide and Conquer," enables students to successfully solve division problems by reaching their answers in a different way—further proof that all students can learn, but all students do not learn in the same way.

Our book also shows you how to provide multiple versions of the same lesson so that students can work independently, at their own level and at their own pace—from learning how to write their names (see "What's in a Name" on page 12) to developing higher-thinking skills (see "Thought Is Taught" on page 83).

A culture is created in the differentiated classroom where students understand that everyone learns in various ways and at various rates. Preserving dignity, providing a safe learning environment, cultivating independence, inspiring trust, encouraging participation, and building community are just a few of the benefits that differentiating instruction can provide. We hope you will keep this handy resource nearby, refer to it often, and soon discover for yourself that by differentiating your instruction, it is truly possible to bring out the best in everyone!

Char Forsten, Gretchen Goodman, Jim Grant, Betty Hollas, and Donna Whyte
2006

► LITERACY ◄

Sentence Puzzles

Introduction

Here is a quick and easy way to create multiple versions of the same lesson so that all children can work at their own level.

Materials

- Sentence strips
- Green, red, and yellow markers
- Business envelopes

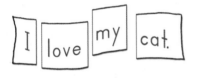

Directions

1. Create a sentence and write it on a sentence strip.
2. Underline the "go" word (first word in the sentence) with the green marker, underline the "stop" sign (punctuation) with the red marker, and underline any popcorn words (remind students that these are high-frequency words) with the yellow marker.

3. Decide how much support each child needs and cut up the sentence strips accordingly. For example:
   - Simply cut the sentence in half for the beginning learner.
   - Cut the sentence apart like a puzzle for the next level of learner.
   - Omit the color coding and cut the sentence apart between the words for higher levels.
4. Put the sentence pieces into an envelope, give it to the student, and have her put the pieces together to form the original sentence.

VARIATION

- For advanced learners, cut the words apart into groups of letters.

GR: K–2

Learning modality:
Visual, kinesthetic

Group size: Individual

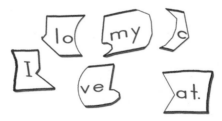

► LITERACY ◄

What's in a Name?

Introduction

Often young children have a difficult time writing their own names. These simple-to-implement exercises will be beneficial to any learner.

Materials

- Yellow highlighter
- White paper

Directions

1. Write the student's name in yellow highlighter on a sheet of paper.
2. Give him the sheet and ask him to trace over the yellow lines with a pencil.
3. Next, print his name using small dots and have him connect the dots to write his name.
4. Then use large, double-lined letters for the student's name and ask him to write the letters of his name inside the lines.
5. When appropriate, ask him to try writing his name on his own.

VARIATION

- Make dotted letters and lined letters of the alphabet ahead of time and photocopy them so that students can cut them out, glue them on paper, and then either connect the dots or color inside the lines.

GR: K–1

Learning modality:
Visual, kinesthetic

Group size: Individual

► LITERACY ◄

Spaghetti and Meatballs

Introduction

When a child makes four or five letters close together, you might assume that he is attempting to write a word when, in fact, each letter may represent a different word to the child. Using spaghetti-and-meatball spaces not only helps children understand the necessity of putting space between letters and words but also allows a teacher to better understand what a child is writing.

Materials

- Orange markers with a thin point
- Brown markers with a thick point

Directions

1. Give each child both types of markers.
2. Model how you want the children to use their markers when they write letters and words:
   - Draw a spaghetti line between letters with the orange marker (pointing out that if there is enough space between the letters, the orange color shouldn't get on either letter).
   - Draw a meatball shape between words to designate a larger space between words.
3. Allow time for the children to practice drawing spaghetti lines and meatball shapes as they write letters and words.

GR: K–1

Learning modality:
Visual, kinesthetic

Group size: Individual

► LITERACY ◄

Roll Call

Introduction

Research suggests that struggling readers and writers share a common denominator a high percentage of the time—they lack phonemic awareness. Here's an easy way to incorporate "playing with sounds" in your classroom.

Directions

1. Change the way you take attendance. Instead of asking, "Is Donna here?" you could say, "Is Onna here?"
2. Then ask your children, "What did I say?" and after they repeat the name as you said it, ask them to fill in the first letter with the correct sound.
3. Next say, "Is Vonna here?"
4. Ask your children again, "What did I say?" and after they repeat what you said, ask them to drop the incorrect sound at the beginning and add a new one to make "Donna."

TIP

- It is important for children to hear both the incorrect and correct sounds, so be sure to continue to ask them, "What did I say?"

GR: K–1

Learning modality: Auditory

Group size: Whole group, small group

► LITERACY ◄

Important to Me Words

Introduction

This activity will help you eliminate lines at your desk at writing time and develop independent writers.

Materials

- Dear Parents letter (see reproducible, page 109)

- Important to Me Words (see reproducible, page 110)

- *My Writing Words* (K–1 and 2–3, see Resources, pages 107–108), or create your own reproducible for a child's personal dictionary

Directions

1. Give the children each a copy of the reproducibles and a copy of *My Writing Words*, or your own reproducible for a child's personal dictionary.

2. Explain to the children that they are to take this material home, give it to a parent or guardian, and work with that individual as described in the letter to parents.

3. Point out to them that there is a date by which they are to bring the material back to class.

4. Have children keep their personal dictionaries in their desks so they are handy during writing time.

Important to Me Words

Mom's name ___Diane___
Dad's name ___Tommy___
The name your child calls his/her grandparents ___Grampy, Honey___
Siblings' name(s) ___Amy, Benjamin, Candice___
Pets' names ___Tess, Chutney, Ollie___
Street you live on ___Fairfield Road___
Town you live in ___Westford___
Favorite color (please write it using that color) ___blue___
Favorite food ___chocolate ice cream___
Favorite show ___Nature___
Favorite book ___Green Eggs and Ham___
Favorite character ___Tigger___
Favorite toy ___Curious George___

Please add any other words that you know are Important to Me words for your child.
___hamburger___
___cereal___
___piano___
___baseball___
___tomorrow___
___crocodile___

TIPS

- Encourage parents of K–1 children to add pictures (real or drawn) to the dictionaries and ask them to write their children's favorite color in the dictionary using that color pen, pencil, or crayon.

- When focusing on high-frequency words, emphasize the importance of spelling these words correctly and have the children highlight them in their personal dictionaries. This way the children can make sure those words that have been worked on by the class are spelled correctly.

GR: K–3

Learning modality: Visual

Group size: Individual

► LITERACY ◄

Color-Coded Encouragement

Introduction

This strategy encourages students of all abilities to participate in shared reading.

Materials

- Poster board
- Repetitive poem or story
- Colored markers

Directions

1. Write the poem or story on poster board, using a different color marker for words that rhyme, repeat, and/or are recognizable to the students. At the 4th - to 6th -grade levels, find text with challenging vocabulary so students can practice word recognition with three- and four-syllable words.
2. Display the poster board where it can easily be seen by all.
3. Read the poem/story aloud with your students. The different colors will help young students or struggling learners "read along" as they come across the words that are familiar to them.

GR: K–6

Learning modality:
Visual, auditory

Group size: Whole group, small group

► LITERACY ◄

Slap and Spell

Introduction

This method of practice provides a hands-on, auditory, kinesthetic approach to help students internalize their spelling words. It is especially helpful for students who have difficulty paying attention and who do not learn well simply by writing spelling words.

Directions

1. Group students in pairs, making sure partners are in the same spelling group or program. (They need to be of similar skills attainment.)
2. Have students face each other, standing about two feet apart, and place their hands in the air, opposite each other's.
3. With a list of spelling words in full view, explain that students are to take turns saying the letters in their spelling words in sequence. As they say a letter, they slap their partner's hand, in a cross-lateral fashion. For example, let's say Student A and Student B are partners. If the word is "bike," Student A says "b" and slaps Student B's opposite, diagonal hand. Then Student B says, "i" and slaps Partner A's opposite, diagonal hand. Next, Student A says and slaps "k" and Student B ends by saying and slapping "e."

VARIATION

*   Students can form a group of two lines standing opposite each other. They practice words as described in the above activity, only they move one partner to the right with each new word to increase the amount of practice.

GR: K–6

Learning modality:
Auditory, kinesthetic, tactile

Group size: Pair

► LITERACY ◄

Walk-Around Punctuation

Introduction

This innovative approach to teaching the rules of punctuation enables your students to not only read them but also see them, hear them, and feel them.

Materials

- Books with short sentences and appropriate punctuation

Directions

1. Provide the students with a variety of books and allow each one to select the book she wants to read.

2. Ask the students to line up about an arm's length from one another and then start walking around the room, whisper reading to themselves as they use the following motions/movements:
   - When they come to a comma, pause briefly, or draw a comma in the air, and then continue walking and reading.
   - When they come to a period, stop completely, and then continue walking and reading.
   - When they come to an exclamation point, do a little hop, or draw an exclamation point in the air, and continue walking and reading.
   - When they come to a question mark, shrug their shoulders, or draw a question mark in the air, and continue walking and reading.
   - When they come to an apostrophe or quotation marks, draw them in the air, and continue walking and reading.

3. Watch your students as they move around the room, starting and stopping and doing hand motions in the air. This kinesthetic exercise will help them internalize rather than simply memorize the rules.

GR: 1–6

Learning modality:
Visual, auditory, kinesthetic

Group size: Small group, whole group

▶ LITERACY ◀

VARIATIONS

- Consider adding sound effects to the motions for added emphasis.

- Adapt this strategy for Walk-Around Editing, where students walk around as they edit. Because they don't see the need for punctuation, they "feel" it through movement.

TIP

- Obtain a copy of the video or DVD of *The Best of Victor Borge*, Acts 1 & 2 (available through music/bookstores as well as online), which is a comic routine of his putting sounds to punctuation marks. Show it to your class and then let them try incorporating the same motions into their walk-arounds.

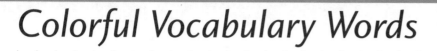

Colorful Vocabulary Words

"Shimmering BLUE"
"Radiant RED"
"Sunshine YELLOW"

Introduction

In differentiated instruction, you want to find different pathways for students to learn and practice skills and concepts. Use the following as a mini-lesson in writing: students take on the roles of naming paint colors as a way of broadening their work with effective adjectives.

Materials

- Paint chips/color samples, individual and multisectioned strips (ask your local hardware/paint store to donate as many as possible)

Directions

1. Cut off or white out the current color names on some of the paint chip strips. Laminate all of the strips for long-term use.
2. Pass out a variety of strips that still have the color name attached.
3. Discuss the creative names of the colors and have students think of new names they would give the colors (shimmering blue, for example).
4. After adequate practice, give students paint chip strips without the color names and tell them they've been hired to name the colors, using effective adjectives.

VARIATIONS

- Use strips that show one color in three different shades. Students can learn superlatives by marking them light/lighter/lightest, green/greener/greenest, etc.

- Have students create their own colored paint chips at the art center, or with the help of the art teacher, and then name their own unique colors.

- Ask students to describe an overall mood or feeling that they associate with the colors. These could change from shade to shade or include only the pastel shade at one end of the strip and the dark shade at the opposite end.

GR: 1–6

Learning modality: Visual

Group size: Pair/triad, individual

▶ LITERACY ◀

Keys to Spelling

Introduction

This hands-on, kinesthetic exercise requires learners to repeatedly "keyboard" their spelling words. Use it as a fun and effective way to get the words into their "motor memory."

Materials

- Keyboards: old or recycled, a photocopy, an overhead transparency, or make your own
- Butcher paper, poster board, or shower curtain liner (optional)
- Flyswatters or Word Whackers [see Resources, pages 107–108] (optional)

Directions

1. Obtain old or recycled keyboards (one per student); make a photocopy of a keyboard for each student; or make an overhead transparency of a keyboard and project the image onto butcher paper, poster board, or a shower curtain liner and trace around the image.
2. Explain that one option for students to practice spelling is to keyboard their words, repeatedly typing them on the keyboard.
3. If students use the large, projected keyboard, they can swat or whack the letters in each word by using flyswatters or Word Whackers.

GR: K–6

Learning modality: Visual, kinesthetic, tactile

Group size: Individual

VARIATIONS

- Provide touchtone phones for spelling practice.
- With the shower curtain liner spread on the floor, let students tap out the words with their feet.
- Kindergartners can use the keyboard to practice the alphabet.

► LITERACY ◄

Stepping Down to the Details

Introduction

This activity builds language skills, teaches students about main ideas and details, and lends itself well to differentiation.

Materials

- Dry-erase board
- Dry-erase markers

Directions

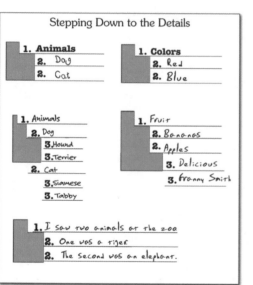

1. On your dry-erase board, copy the example shown (see illustration).

2. Explain to students that step #2 is always an example, description, or subcategory of step #1 and step #3 is always an example, description, or subcategory of step #2, and so forth. (Dog and cat are examples of animals; hound and terrier are examples of dogs; Siamese and tabby are examples of cats.)

3. When a filler or sponge activity is needed, make a sheet similar to the illustration shown here. Write a different word, category, or concept on the top lines (1.) and ask your students to outline these, breaking them down into greater details.

VARIATIONS

- Create and make copies of a number of these ahead of time so you have them to use at a moment's notice.

- Differentiate by asking higher-level students to complete sentences and paragraphs.

TIP

- Give younger students examples with only two levels, such as animals: dog, cat.

GR: 3–6

Learning modality:
Visual

Group size: Any

► LITERACY ◄

Word Work

Introduction

Often students are asked to make small words from the letters in bigger vocabulary words. Here is a way to ensure success for all students.

Materials

- Letter squares, approximately 1 inch (homemade or purchased)
- Resealable plastic bags

Directions

1. Write a vocabulary word at the top of a sheet of paper and make a copy for each student.
2. Using the letter squares, enclose all the letters for that word in resealable bags. Fill enough bags so that each student has one.
3. Distribute the vocabulary word sheets and letter bags to your students.
4. Have students empty their bags and then rearrange the letters into a smaller word.
5. Tell students to write their new word on their paper, put the letters back into the bag, toss them around, and then begin again, making a new word, writing it down, returning letters to the bag, and so forth.

TIP

- Start small by having the learner find/make only three to four words from a larger word.

GR: 1–4

Learning modality:
Visual, kinesthetic, tactile

Group size: Individual

▶ LITERACY ◀

Mumble Reading

Introduction

Mumble reading is a technique that can help students build persistence when reading unfamiliar or difficult text. As they speak into the whisper/phonics phone, they literally hear themselves trying to figure out new words and making approximations, and this will encourage them to persevere.

Materials

- Whisper/phonics phone (see Resources, pages 107–108) for each student

Directions

1. Project a text using the overhead and model how you read and make approximations as you try to figure out the words.
2. Show how to stretch out a word while sounding out its various parts.
3. Distribute whisper/phonics phones to the students and allow time for them to practice reading an appropriate text.
4. Explain that they are to go back and self-correct should they realize the word they sounded out doesn't make sense in the context of the sentence.

GR: 1–4

Learning modality:
Visual, auditory

Group size: Individual

► **LITERACY** ◄

Start Your Engines

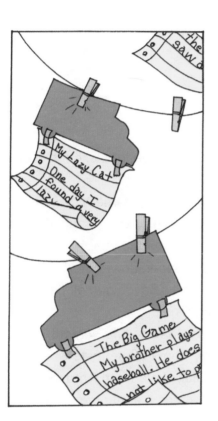

Introduction

Often students are given a specific writing prompt on statewide assessments and asked to complete the story. The following activity prepares students for that task, as well as motivates them to do their best initial writing since their work will be used by their peers.

Materials

• Construction paper

• Truck template (see reproducible, page 111), one for each student

• Clothes rack or clothesline

• Clothespins

Directions

1. Distribute a sheet of construction paper and a truck template to each student.

2. Have the students trace around the template onto the construction paper and then cut out their truck shape.

3. Spend some time brainstorming ideas with your students about ways to begin a story. Include examples such as questions, exclamations, or statements.

4. Ask the students to take a sheet of writing paper and begin a story about a topic of their choice (pets, sports team, family vacation, weather disaster, etc.). Make sure they understand they are writing only the beginning—a story starter—not the entire story.

5. Allow them to write for two or three minutes and then have them tape or glue their story starter to their truck shape.

6. Ask them to attach their trucks to the clothes rack or clothesline with clothespins.

7. In the next few days, challenge students to take a truck that does not have their own writing, start their engines, and continue the story.

GR: 2–4

Learning modality:
Visual, tactile

Group size: Whole group

► LITERACY ◄

Trees of Thought

Introduction

This activity can become a permanent part of a bulletin board.

Materials

- Brown and green construction paper, plus any other colors desired
- Marker
- Push pins

Directions

1. Using the brown construction paper, draw two tree trunks, each with many branches but no leaves.
2. Laminate the paper, cut out the trees, and label one tree "fiction" and the other "nonfiction." Attach both to the bulletin board. (Laminate so the tasks can be varied and changed throughout the year.)
3. Using the remaining colors of construction paper, draw a number of leaves, laminate them, and cut out each one. (Save yourself time by having each student cut out 5 to 10 leaves.)
4. Write a variety of familiar book titles on the leaves, one per leaf.
5. Distribute leaves to the students and ask them to determine whether their titles are for fiction or nonfiction books. Have them write their initials on the bottom of their leaves and attach them to the correct tree using pushpins.
6. Change the task weekly and watch the trees grow and fill.

VARIATIONS

- For younger students, label one tree "odd" and the other "even." Ask students to write a number on each of their leaves and attach them to the correct tree.

- For 4th to 6th graders, a tree trunk could be made for each genre being taught and then book titles (leaves) could be put on the trees throughout the year. For example, genres might include historical fiction, fantasy, realistic fiction, mystery, etc.

GR: K–6

Learning modality:
Visual, tactile

Group size: Any

► LITERACY ◄

Take a Chance on Spelling

Introduction

This strategy not only encourages participation but also allows you to address the specific spelling needs of each child.

Materials

- Sticky notes or small white boards or chalkboards

Directions

1. Create "safe" ways for students to "take a chance" on spelling unknown words by providing them with sticky notes or a small white board or chalkboard.
2. During writing time, tell students not to ask you how to spell a word unless they have tried to do it themselves first on their notes or boards.
3. After they have tried spelling the word on their own, have them show you what they have written so you can check it. Then tell them they can write the final version on their papers.

TIP

- When students are unsure of the correct spelling, they often think of two or three possibilities, so encourage them to write down each one. This increases their awareness of vowels and of the various sounds they make as well as spelling rules.

GR: 1–6

Learning modality:
Visual, auditory, kinesthetic

Group size: Whole group, small group

► LITERACY ◄

Climb the Word Ladder

Introduction

Word Ladders require minimal preparation but provide an opportunity for meaningful independent work. Use them as a sponge activity to build and reinforce vocabulary and spelling.

Materials
- Word Ladder (see reproducible, page 112)

Directions

1. On a copy of the reproducible, write a word on the first step of the Word Ladder.
2. Make copies of the reproducible with the one word entered; give the copies to your students.
3. Explain that each student is to start with the word on the first step of the ladder and change one letter to create a new word for the second step. So if the first word is "step," the second word might be "stop."
4. Tell the students to continue up the ladder, changing one letter on each step and seeing how high they can go.

VARIATIONS

- To create a more challenging Word Ladder, start with a more difficult word.

- Another way to differentiate for higher-level students is to have them alternate between changing a letter (or letters) and adding a letter (or letters). For example, if the first word is "stop," the second word might be "step," and the third word might be "steep."

TIP

- The first time you do this activity, use a ladder with only a few steps, and then gradually increase the number of steps.

GR: 2–6

Learning modality: Visual

Group size: Individual

28

► LITERACY ◄

Thinking Inside the Box

Introduction

Use this activity after a reading assignment or even after watching a video. It helps students build on prior knowledge and enables students of any level to answer questions.

Materials

- 9-inch square piece of paper, one per student

Directions

1. Give each student a paper square.
2. Ask the students to fold their paper in half and then in half again, creating a sheet with four equal-size boxes.
3. Determine how you want the learner to respond, and then provide students with a variety of response "starters" on the board. Examples should range from simpler choices, such as "I think…," "I wonder…," "This reminds me of…," and "I feel…," to higher-level choices, such as "The ending should be changed to…," "I could apply this knowledge to…," "I can compare and contrast this story to…," and "If this story took place in the 1800s, it would…."
4. Have students select four response starters, write one in each box on their paper, and then write their response to each one in the appropriate box.

"I think:"…
the owners should have taken Pogo with them on vacation

"I wonder:"…
how the dog felt when his owners left

"This reminds me of:"…
the time I stayed at Nana's when mom and dad went to Hawaii

"I feel:"…
So sorry for Pogo that I could cry

GR: 3–6

Learning modality: Visual, tactile

Group size: Any

VARIATION

- When first using this activity, assign the quotes you want the students to respond to.

► LITERACY ◄

Personalizing Parts of Speech

Introduction

This strategy helps students learn parts of speech by making a personal connection when possible.

Materials

- Personalizing Parts of Speech (see reproducible, page 113)

Directions

1. Distribute a copy of the reproducible to each student. (The sheets can be attached to a folder and kept in the student's desk.)
2. Direct students to label each part of speech and include one or two personal examples that describe that part of speech where it is possible to do so.

VARIATION

- Omit the names, mix up the sheets, distribute to the students, and have them try to find the owner.

GR: 4–6

Learning modality: Visual

Group size: Individual

```
Name  Aimee _____

Noun: _actress, teacher____
Pronoun: _she, me_____
Verb: _runs_____
Adjective: _dramatic, happy_
Adverb: _slowly_____
Conjunction: _and_____
Preposition: _on, in_____
Article: _the, a_____
```

Sentence Stretcher

Introduction
This game challenges students to make their writing more descriptive and interesting.

Materials
- Chalk or markers of two colors

Directions
1. Divide the class into two teams—Team A and Team B—and give both teams a different color chalk or marker.
2. Write a sentence on the board, such as "The boy rode a horse."
3. Ask Team A to add one word to the sentence. For example, a team member might insert the word "confidently" after "boy": "The boy confidently rode a horse."
4. Ask Team B to add another word. They might insert "galloping" before "horse": "The boy confidently rode a galloping horse."
5. Continue until neither team can think of another word to add.
6. Count up the colored responses from each team to determine who wins that round, and repeat for another round or more.

TIP
- Give extra points for correct spelling.

GR: 3–6

Learning modality:
Visual, kinesthetic

Group size: Whole group, small group

Clipped Speech

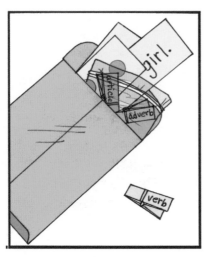

Introduction

Generally, words are classified according to eight parts of speech. Students who need practice labeling parts of speech will benefit from this hands-on exercise, which can be used in small groups or individually.

Materials

- 10–15 sentence strips
- Permanent markers (red, pink, yellow, green, blue, orange, purple, black)
- 40 or more colored, snap clothespins (or wooden ones colored with permanent marker)
- Large manila envelope
- Resealable plastic bag

Directions

1. Write a sentence on each of the sentence strips. On the back of each and at the appropriate spot, place a colored dot (see step #2) to signify if the word on the front is a noun, verb, etc., to allow for self-checking.
2. Label the colored clothespins as follows: red—noun; pink—pronoun; yellow—verb; green—adjective; blue—adverb; orange—preposition; purple—conjunction; black—article.
3. Place the sentence strips inside the manila envelope and enclose a resealable plastic bag filled with clothespins.
4. Give a student the envelope and tell her to take out a sentence strip and attach colored clothespins to it at the appropriate parts of speech.
5. When finished, have her turn the sentence strip over and check her work. Tell her to continue the same procedure with the remaining strips.

GR: 4–6

Learning modality:
Visual, tactile

Group size: Small group, individual

6. Have students share the sentence they found to be the most challenging.

TIP

• Make sure to space the words in the sentences so there's room for each clothespin to be attached.

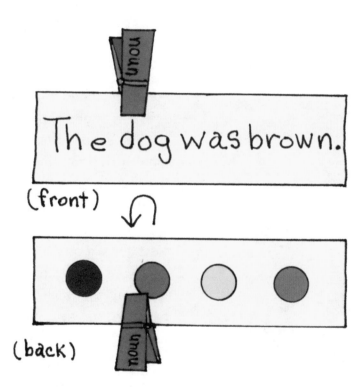

► LITERACY ◄

SQ3R

Introduction

This popular strategy for helping students comprehend and make sense of difficult text has been successfully used since the 1940s, when F. P. Robinson coined the acronym in a book entitled Effective Study. *It embraces three important aspects of reading: prereading, during reading, and after reading.*

Materials

- SQ3R poster (see reproducible, page 114)
- SQ3R bookmark (see reproducible, page 115)

Directions

1. Make an overhead transparency of the poster reproducible.
2. Make an enlarged copy of the poster reproducible, laminate it, and place it in a prominent part of your classroom, where all students can read it easily.
3. Make multiple copies of the bookmark reproducible, laminate them, cut them out as individual bookmarks, and distribute one to each student.
4. Project the text on the overhead.
5. Explicitly model (or "think aloud" for your students) how to do each step in the SQ3R. For example, talk to them about what it means to "survey" a text and then actually model how this is done, using a piece of text.
6. Encourage students to whisper read as they do the SQ3R steps and to use procedural self-talk.

SQ3R

S 1st Survey the passage to be read.

Q 2nd Create questions from headings and subheadings.

R 3rd Read the passage to answer the questions you have developed.

R 4th Recite by creating an oral or written summarization of what has been read.

R 5th Review by answering the questions created for the passage.

GR: 4–6

Learning modality:
Visual, auditory

Group size: Individual

VARIATION

- Instead of whisper reading, students could write down some words that stand out and might give clues to the content.

TIP

- Make photocopies of the bookmark on different colored paper.

▶ MATH ◀

When Was That?

Introduction

Some students have difficulty telling time and grasping the concept of lapses of time, such as "in 15 minutes" or "15 minutes ago." This hands-on activity helps eliminate confusion.

Materials

- Clock face and hands (see reproducible, page 116)
- Brass brads

Directions

1. Make enough copies of the reproducibles so that each student plus you will have a completed clock.
2. Cut out the clock faces and hands and attach the hands to the clocks with brass brads.
3. Distribute a completed clock to each student.
4. Hold up your clock in front of the room, set the hands to a specific time, and state what the time is. Ask the students to set their clocks for the same time. Check for accuracy and repeat these steps nine more times, setting the clock differently each time.
5. Set your clock for a different time and have the students figure what the time will be in 5 minutes. Check the students' clocks again and repeat nine more times.
6. Move to the next level by asking what time it will be in 10 minutes, and repeat nine more times.
7. The final step of this task is having the students figure what the time was 5 minutes ago, 10 minutes ago, and so forth.

GR: 1–3

Learning modality:
Visual, tactile

Group size: Whole group, small group, individual

►MATH◄

Give 'Em a Hand

Introduction

Your students will appreciate this "handy" method for understanding the concept of measurement.

Materials

- Card stock or oak tag for tracing hands
- Index cards (prepared as described)

Directions

1. Have each student trace around one of her hands and write her name on it.
2. Laminate the hands, cut them out, and put them at a math center in a basket labeled "Handfuls."
3. Model for the students how to measure with a hand—from the tip of the middle finger to the bottom of the palm (see illustration).
4. On separate index cards, write specific tasks for students to complete at the center, such as:

   - Find something in the front of the room that measures three of John's hands.
   - Find something in the classroom that is shorter than Albert's hand.
   - Locate five items in the coat closet that are smaller than Maisie's hand.

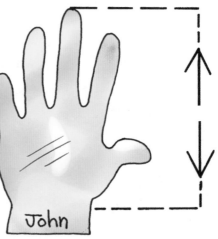

GR: 1–3

Learning modality: Visual, kinesthetic, tactile

Group size: Small group

► MATH ◄

Ticket Digits

Introduction

Students often tire of math problems when they are always presented in the same way, so this activity gives them something more than just paper and pencil to work with.

Materials

- Roll of carnival/movie tickets (available from office supply stores)
- Calculators

Directions

1. Distribute one ticket and a blank piece of paper to each student.
2. Direct the students to add up the digits on their ticket, using the paper as their work sheet. For example, if the number on a student's ticket (let's call him Nick) is 760134, he will add those six digits together and write the total (21) on his work sheet.
3. Next, have students write their name on the back of their ticket and pass the ticket to another student.
4. Ask students to add up the digits on the new ticket they were handed and write the answer on their papers. For example, if Nick gave his ticket to Jennifer, she would add up the same digits (760134) and write the total on her work sheet.
5. Have students compare their answers to those of the student who gave them the ticket. (Nick and Jennifer would compare their totals for the ticket marked with 760134 to see if they got the same answer.)
6. Let students check their answers with a calculator.

GR: 2–4

Learning modality:
Visual, auditory, kinesthetic, tactile

Group size: Whole group, small group

► MATH ◄

Multiplication Mix-Ups

Introduction

In a typical classroom, there are often students who struggle to memorize basic multiplication facts. The following method breaks the memorization process down into more manageable chunks or parts, so students don't feel overwhelmed.

Materials

• Large chart with multiplication facts on them (optional)

Directions

1. Begin by teaching the multiplication facts for x 0 and for x 1 since these are the easiest for students to grasp. Practice and review these until they are mastered. For some children, this may take one period, for others, one week.

2. Next, teach the x 2 facts, followed by the x 5 facts, and then same numbers (3 x 3, 4 x 4, etc.). Again, be sure students have mastered each set of facts before moving on. (Since this is an individual or small group activity, the children who have mastered their math facts will be working at their own level on assigned tasks, such as work sheets or activities in the math center.)

3. Next, teach the x 9 facts. Note, however, that students will only need to learn 9 x 3, 9 x 4, 9 x 6, 9 x 7, and 9 x 8, as you've already taught them 9 x 0, 9 x 1, 9 x 2, and 9 x 5.

4. Once students feel success, they are more able to master the remaining facts.

GR: 2–3

Learning modality:
Visual

Group size: Small group, individual

▶ MATH ◀

Put It in Its Place!

Introduction

Help your students grasp the concept of place value with this interactive strategy.

Materials

- Library pockets (available from office supply stores), four for each student

- One folder for each student

- 2–4 sets of index cards, numbered 0 through 9, for each student

Directions

1. Attach four pockets to the inside of each folder. Label the pockets Thousands, Hundreds, Tens, Ones (see illustration).
2. If you are teaching and reviewing only tens and ones, give students only two sets each of the numbered index cards; otherwise, give each student four sets.
3. Call out a number, such as 472, and have the students place their cards in the correct pockets. Remind them to insert the cards so that the numbers can be seen.
4. Ask the students to hold up their folders and show their responses.

GR: 2–4

Learning modality: Visual, kinesthetic, tactile

Group size: Whole group, small group

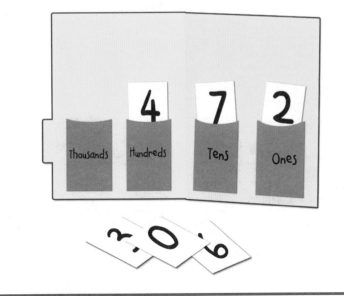

►MATH◄

Spread It Out

Introduction

Students who learn differently can benefit from an alternate approach. This is a simple way to help students understand addition through expanded mathematical notation.

Materials

- Paper and pencils or dry-erase boards and markers

$$34 = 3 \text{ tens} + 4 \text{ ones}$$
$$+28 = 2 \text{ tens} + 8 \text{ ones}$$
$$\overline{ 5 \text{ tens} + 12 \text{ ones}}$$

$$12 \text{ ones} = 1 \text{ ten} + 2 \text{ ones}$$
$$\overline{\phantom{12 \text{ ones} = } 6 \text{ tens} + 2 \text{ ones}}$$
$$62$$

Directions

1. Help the student understand how to break apart double-digit numbers. For example, 34 = 3 tens and 4 ones.
2. Go no further until the student has mastered that.
3. Next, begin with a simple double-digit addition problem, such as:

   34 + 28

   34 = 3 tens and 4 ones
   28 = 2 tens and 8 ones

   Add the ones first:
   4 ones and 8 ones is 12 ones
   3 tens and 2 tens is 5 tens

   Regroup the ones so that it is now 2 ones and 1 ten. Place the extra ten with the 5 tens to have 6 tens and 2 ones, or 62.

VARIATION

- Use Place Value Strips, Disks, and/or Cubes (see Resources, pages 107–108) for further demonstration.

GR: 2–5

Learning modality: Visual

Group size: Individual

► MATH ◄

Tennis, Anyone?

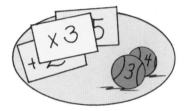

Introduction

Here's an active and engaging way to reach all learners when teaching addition and multiplication facts.

Materials

- 11 dead tennis balls (check with local clubs or fitness centers)

Directions

1. Write a number from 0 to 10 on each ball.
2. Assemble multiplication fact cards from x 0 to x 10; for younger students, use addition facts instead of multiplication.
3. Have students stand or sit in a large circle, and display the number fact for the activity, such as x 3 or + 3.
4. Beginning with only five tennis balls, toss or roll the balls to students in the circle. As soon as they catch a ball, their task is to figure out the math fact and be prepared to give the answer. So, if a student catches a ball with 6 on it, he should answer "18" or "9," respectively.

GR: 1–4

Learning modality:
Kinesthetic

Group size: Whole group, small group

The Vast Array

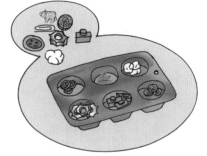

Introduction

Using manipulatives enables students to more easily see that multiplication is a quick way to do addition and division is a quick way to do subtraction.

Materials

*   Counting chips, pennies, Mini-Pigs (see Resources, pages 107–108), buttons, bolts, cotton balls, or other similar small items
*   Egg cartons, muffin tins, ice cube trays, nail/screw organizers, or anything with mini-compartments in rows and/or columns

Directions

1. Give each student an even number of small items plus a container with mini-compartments.
2. Direct the students to distribute their items equally among the compartments in their container. For example, if the student has 12 chips and an egg carton, she could put 4 chips in 3 of the egg carton cups to represent $4 \times 3 = 12$; or 2 chips in 6 of the egg carton cups to represent $2 \times 6 = 12$; etc.
3. Use the containers also to teach division. Show that 18 chips divided equally among 6 sections equals 3: $18 \div 6 = 3$

VARIATION

*   With students in pairs or small groups, use a number that has many multiples, 30 for example, and have students show the various multiplication facts that would equal that number, such as 1×30, 2×15, 3×10, and 5×6.

TIP

*   To make this simpler on yourself, have students bring in their own array of items.

GR: 2–3

Learning modality:
Visual, kinesthetic, tactile

Group size: Any

►MATH◄

Gallon Master

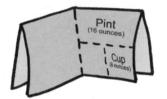

Introduction

Teaching students the equivalent amounts for cups, pints, quarts, and gallons can be challenging, but it doesn't need to be if you use this simple paper-folding activity.

Materials

• Gallon Master (see reproducible, pages 117–118), one per student
• Liquid measure containers for gallon, quart, pint, and cup

Directions

1. Distribute a copy of the reproducible to each student.
2. Model how the reproducible, which represents a gallon (128 ounces), is folded in half to create a half gallon (64 ounces), folded in half again to represent a quart (32 ounces), folded in half again to represent a pint (16 ounces), and so forth.
3. Provide time for students to fold, unfold, and refold their copies of the Gallon Master, which offers visual, kinesthetic, and tactile practice and reinforcement.
4. Next, show students a gallon of liquid and demonstrate how it divides into equivalent amounts as you pour from the large container into smaller ones.

VARIATION

• Use this same strategy to teach the metric system.

GR: 2–6

Learning modality:
Visual, kinesthetic, tactile

Group size: Individual

►MATH◄

Here's the Answer, What's the Question?

Introduction

This ideal sponge activity invites everyone to participate because there is no one correct answer.

Directions

1. On a section of your bulletin board, post five numbers (such as 15, 8, 4, 20, 7).
2. Tell your students that the numbers are answers and you want them to write one or more questions for each one. Point out, perhaps, that one of them needs to be a word problem. For example, if a student chose 15, she might write, "What is half of 30?" or "How much is 14 + 1?"
3. If desired, have students do their work in a journal instead of handing in papers.

GR: 2–6

Learning modality: Visual

Group size: Pairs, individual

VARIATION

• Post words from content areas and tell students that these are the answers, and you want to know what the questions are. For example, answers could be Abraham Lincoln, Emancipation Proclamation, Robert E. Lee, Appomattox, Ulysses S. Grant. Questions could be, "Who was president of the United States during the Civil War?" and "Who led the Confederate army during the Civil War?"

Top Hat Math

Introduction

This word-problem anchor activity provides meaningful practice for all students.

Materials

- 5 x 8-inch index cards
- Hat for holding cards

Directions

1. Distribute index cards to the students.
2. Assign each student the task of writing her own word problem and its step-by-step solution on the back of the index card.
3. Gather the cards and place them in a hat labeled Math Hat.
4. Later, when you need a time-filler or students are asking what they can do, bring out the Math Hat and invite a student to remove a card from it.
5. Assign the class the task of completing the problem. Students will enjoy having their work displayed and tackled by others.

GR: 4–6

Learning modality: Visual

Group size: Whole group, small group

►MATH◄

Division Procedure

Introduction

Division requires students to know the sequence of the steps involved. To help struggling students stay on track and keep from becoming confused and discouraged, make a poster of the steps for your classroom and distribute bookmarks showing the steps as well.

Materials

- 6 Division Steps poster (see reproducible, page 119)
- 6 Division Steps bookmark (see reproducible, page 120)
- Good Luck with Your Division! (see reproducible, page 121)
- Sticky notes

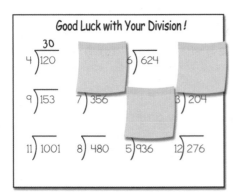

Directions

1. Make an enlarged copy of the poster, laminate it, and post it in an easy-to-see location in the classroom.
2. Make multiple photocopies of the bookmark, laminate them, and cut them into individual bookmarks, making enough so each student will have one.
3. Fill in a set of division problems on the Good Luck with Your Division! sheet and make a copy for each student.
4. Give each student a copy of the sheet, a bookmark, and some blank sticky notes.
5. Demonstrate on the Good Luck with Your Division! sheet how to arrange blank sticky notes around a single math problem so students can focus on only one at a time, if desired.
6. Allow students time to complete their sheets.

GR: 4–6
Learning modality:
Visual, auditory, tactile
Group size: Individual

TIP

- Encourage students to talk aloud when doing long division, which provides them with an internal support system.

►MATH◄

Circulation Problems

Introduction

Use this versatile activity across the curriculum as a small-group or whole-class review.

Materials

- Math problems sheet (prepared as described), one per student
- Index cards (prepared as described)

Directions

1. On a sheet of paper, write out a number of math problems that you want your students to solve, and then write the answer for each one on separate index cards.
2. Give each student a copy of the math sheet and tape one of the index cards to the back of each student.
3. Provide time for the students to solve the problems and then instruct them to walk around the room with their math sheets and look for the answers to each of the math problems.
4. When they find the match, they write the name of the student who is "wearing" the correct answer on their math sheets, followed by the answer. For example, if one of the math problems is "8 x 8" and Jodell is wearing "64," the student who finds this match writes: "Jodell — 64"
5. Continue until the students match up all the math problems with their answers, or for as long as you prefer.

GR: 4–6

Learning modality:
Visual, kinesthetic

Group size: Whole group, small group

VARIATIONS

- This also works well with vocabulary words and their definitions: "Volcano," "Charlie — a large mountain containing lava and ash"

- Use with reading comprehension questions about the book the class is reading, or with geography or science content questions based on the unit of study.

►MATH◄

Divide and Conquer

Introduction

Some students may understand the concept of division but have difficulty with number sense or math facts. Using the following method, these students can still be successful solving division problems; they simply reach their answers in a different way.

Directions

1. On a sheet of blank paper, draw a vertical line down the center of the page, creating two columns. At the top of the left-hand column, write a division problem such as 20 ÷ 5 (see illustration).

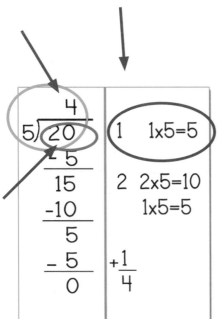

2. Give the sheet to a student who is struggling with division and ask her to look at the problem and decide if she can get at least 1 group of 5 out of 20.

3. If she says yes, show her how to indicate this: she writes the number 1 in the right-hand column across from the problem (see illustration), and then multiplies 1 x 5 , which is 5, and writes the 5 under the 20 in the problem in the left-hand column. She subtracts 5 from 20, which leaves 15 (see illustration).

4. Ask her the same question again: can she get at least 1 more group of 5 out of 15? Looking at the 15, she decides she can get at least 2 groups of 5, so she writes 2 in the right-hand column, under the 1, multiplies 2 x 5, which is 10, and writes 10 under the 15 in the left-hand column. She subtracts 10 from 15 and gets 5.

GR: 3–6

Learning modality:
Visual

Group size: Individual

5. She knows there is 1 group of 5 in 5, so she writes 1 in the right-hand column under the 2, multiplies 1 x 5, which is 5, and writes 5 under the 5 in the left-hand column. She subtracts 5 from 5 and gets 0.

►MATH◄

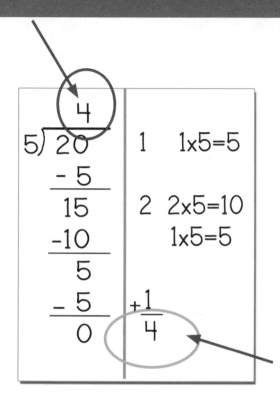

6. Now, she adds up the numbers in the right-hand column (1 + 2 + 1 = 4), which gives her the number of groups of 5 that are in 20, which is 4. She then writes this number (the quotient) in the division problem at the top of the left-hand column.

7. What she is learning is that division is repeated subtraction (20 − 5 − 10 − 5).

8. With this method, the student is reaching the same answer as everyone else, but she's learning a different way to divide and conquer!

TIP

• A number does not always need to be divided by 1 group at a time. If you ask a student to use this strategy, he might start with 1 group but then realize that the number has at least 2 groups or 3 groups.

► MATH ◄

Are You Worth a Million?

Introduction

This sponge activity helps early finishers soak up extra minutes when there isn't enough time left for a full lesson. You can change the activity every day or every week, depending on how often you want to use it.

Materials

- Are You Worth a Million? sheet (see reproducible, page 122)
- Calculator (optional)

Directions

1. Make copies of the reproducible and distribute to those students who need to fill some time.

2. Have students print their first names, find the value of each letter, and multiply the values together. Allow students to use a calculator when appropriate.

3. Have students address the question, "Are you worth a million?" If their first names do not equal a million, have them follow the same steps with their middle names, and add that value to their first names.

4. Have them check again, "Are you worth a million?" If not, they repeat the procedure with their last names.

5. For those who still are not worth a million, have them use the guess-and-check method of problem-solving to come up with a name that is worth exactly a million.

GR: 3–6

Learning modality:
Visual, kinesthetic

Group size: Individual

VARIATIONS

- Use this with language arts. For example, ask students to come up with five nouns, each of which has letter values that add up to exactly 15.

- Using science words, ask students to find four words that, when multiplied together, come to exactly 50.

►COMMUNITY BUILDING◄

Jewel Boxes

Introduction

A sense of community is important in a differentiated classroom. Be sure to recognize and celebrate the individual student's progress, accomplishments, and achievements in addition to those of the whole class. Using Jewel Boxes helps realize these goals and keeps students organized.

Materials

- Cardboard school box for each student
- Nontoxic gold spray paint
- Jewels (bags of colored pieces, available in craft stores)
- Glue for each student

Directions

1. Spray paint each box gold.
2. Give students their own boxes to use for storing items such as scissors, crayons, pencils, glue, etc.
3. Show students the "jewels" and tell them that there are ways the entire class can earn jewels for their boxes. For example, if another teacher or the principal compliments the class, every student earns a jewel.
4. Explain that they can earn jewels individually as well. For example, if a particular student improves behavior, reaches an academic goal, etc., he can receive a jewel to decorate his box.
5. Allow students to decorate their boxes however they want.

VARIATIONS

- Each side of the box could be designated for something specific, such as a side for reaching goals in math or in spelling, for good behavior, etc.

GR: K–3

Learning modality:
Visual, auditory, kinesthetic, tactile

Group size: Whole group, small group, individual

► COMMUNITY BUILDING ◄

Take a Stand

Introduction

This is a simple way to engage students with others who think like they do. It provides a chance for movement, interaction, and group responses. Students are more likely to take a stand in this manner than by raising their hands.

Materials

- Construction paper of different colors

Directions

1. Draw three to five large foot shapes on the construction paper, laminate them, and cut out each one.
2. Write a response or answer on each of the foot shapes. For example, with younger children, you might put a picture of a zoo animal and its name on each foot. For older students, you might write the names Rosa Parks, Martin Luther King, Jr., Bill Clinton, and John F. Kennedy.
3. Read each response to the students before hanging the foot shapes in various places in the classroom.
4. With younger students, you might read a story about zoo animals and then have them "take a stand" and go to the picture of the zoo animal that they think was the bravest or the smartest or the kindest in the story. For older students, lead a discussion about the subject you are teaching and then make a statement, such as, "In my opinion, the person who most impacted the 20th century is…." Tell students to stand next to the foot that they feel best represents their opinion, and then to share their reasons with the others in their group.
5. Next, have students share their responses with the entire class by explaining their opinions.

GR: K–6

Learning modality:
Visual, auditory, kinesthetic

Group size: Whole group

►COMMUNITY BUILDING◄

Seven Dwarfs

Introduction
This exercise demonstrates to students the benefit of collaborating with peers and shows that when they work together as a team, they learn more.

Materials
- Illustration of the Seven Dwarfs
- Music to the song "Hi Ho"

Directions
1. Have students number 1 to 7 on a piece of paper.
2. Display the illustration and ask the students to write the names of the seven dwarfs. Give them about two minutes to do this and play the "Hi Ho" song as they work.
3. When the time is up, ask the students to stand if they've written the seven names. Count the number standing; there may be two or three.
4. Now tell them you're going to give them two more minutes to do this again, but this time you want the students to work collaboratively in groups.
5. After the time is up, ask the students to stand if they have written the seven names. Virtually everybody will get up.
6. Make your point: We all learn more when we work together.

TIP
- Just in case you can't remember their names, the Seven Dwarfs are: Doc, Dopey, Grumpy, Bashful, Happy, Sleepy, and Sneezy.

GR: 2–6

Learning modality:
Visual, auditory

Group size: Whole group, small group, pair/ triad

►COMMUNITY BUILDING◄

Me Map

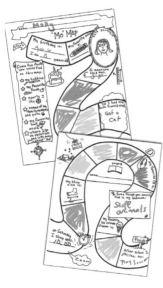

Introduction

This is a great way to start the year and to help students get to know one another and learn more about you (and you about them). It serves as an assessment tool, too!

Materials

- Me Map directions (see reproducible, page 123) for each student
- Me Map (see reproducible, pages 124–125) for younger students
- Poster board
- Markers
- Stickers

Directions

1. Model a Me Map by completing one of your own life and sharing it with your students. They will love learning about you as more than just their teacher.
2. Give each student a copy of the Me Map directions, plus poster board, markers, and stickers. Provide younger students with the Me Map reproducible.
3. Assign a date by which the maps must be completed.
4. Suggest to older students that they first sketch a draft of their maps so they can develop ideas before making their final versions. Emphasize that their maps should be completed with lots of care and thought put into the use of color, icons, and handwriting.

VARIATION

- Give extra credit to those willing to share their maps with the class.

GR: 2–6

Learning modality:
Visual, auditory, kinesthetic, tactile

Group size: Individual

▶ COMMUNITY BUILDING ◀

License to Learn

Introduction

Many people use their vanity license plates to inform other drivers about their professions, interests, or hobbies. This activity requires students to think along those same lines and highlights their individual interests.

Materials

- Overhead transparencies of personal license plates
- Sheets of paper about the size of a license plate, one for each student

Directions

1. On an overhead, display a variety of personal license plates, such as "4n6ngnr" (forensics engineer), "videoma," and "IBPOPPY."
2. Allow students time to brainstorm ideas for their own plates to prevent anyone from getting "stuck."
3. Give students a license plate sheet of paper and ask them to design their own plates, using no more than seven symbols that describe them. Tell them not to show their plates to anyone and to keep their work covered.
4. Gather all the students' plates, select one, and hold it up for the class to see. Ask students what it says and means, and then whom it describes.
5. Select another student's license plate and do the same. You can continue with all the rest or spread this out over a period of days.

VARIATION

- Post the plates on your bulletin board and use them as a fun "Open House" activity for parents as they try to figure out which plate belongs to their child.

TIP

- Allow students to use the plate created during class as a "draft," and later provide them time to create a more "finished" product.

GR: 2–6

Learning modality: Visual, kinesthetic

Group size: Whole group

►COMMUNITY BUILDING◄

The Places I Will Go

Introduction

This is an appealing activity for the whole class. It provides students with a break from the "curriculum express" and an opportunity to learn who their classmates are.

Materials

- *The Places I Will Go* by Dr. Seuss
- Business envelopes

Directions

1. Share the book with your students.
2. Ask the class to project where they think they will be in 20 years. Where will they live? What job might they have? Who will their friends be? How will they help others?
3. Next, have the students write a self-projected story based on their answers, but tell them not to put their names on the stories.
4. Place each story in a sealed envelope and store them in a box or basket in an easily accessible location.
5. When the time is appropriate, direct your students (or an individual) to select and open a sealed envelope, read the story inside, and make a guess about who it is.
6. Have them respond in writing why they think it is that person and then give you their responses.
7. During the day, invite them to discuss what they read and how they came to their conclusions.

GR: 3–6

Learning modality: Visual, auditory, kinesthetic, tactile

Group size: Whole group

TIPS

- Give students time to brainstorm as they think about their futures so they can hear other students' ideas.
- Suggest that students also include an illustration with their personal stories.
- If appropriate, stretch this out over a period of two to four days.

►COMMUNITY BUILDING◄

All About Me (Using Bloom's Taxonomy)

Introduction

This is a get-to-know-you activity that can also serve as an assessment of student likes, dislikes, and interests. In a differentiated classroom, assessment is a key component.

Materials

- All About Me (see reproducible, page 126)

Directions

1. Give each student a copy of the reproducible and explain the six different levels of thinking upon which it is based.
   a. Knowledge—name the information
   b. Comprehension—understand the information
   c. Application—apply the information
   d. Analysis—break the information apart
   e. Synthesis—create something new
   f. Evaluation—judge the information
2. Model how to respond to the various statements by doing one about yourself. Students enjoy getting to know their teacher as a real person!
3. Invite students to write their answers in their journals or on their own paper. You might assign this as homework or as a project to be completed at the end of a week.
4. Once students have completed the activity, consider taking a few minutes at the end of each day to have a student share his work.
5. Collect the work and use it to assess student likes, dislikes, and interests.

VARIATIONS

- Let students choose one response from each level of thinking.
- Let students share their work in small groups.

GR: 4–6

Learning modality: Visual

Group size: Whole group, small group, individual

► ASSESSMENT ◄

Story Cubes

Introduction

This cube activity requires students to think at all levels of Bloom's taxonomy and is popular in a differentiated classroom. Students are asked to respond to different tasks after reading a narrative.

Materials

- Cube template (see reproducible, page 127)
- Card stock or heavy paper
- Bloom's Cube literature sheet (see reproducible, page 128)

Directions

1. Make photocopies of the cube template onto card stock or heavy paper, so each student or group of students will have a cube.
2. Select and write one question or statement from Bloom's Cube literature sheet on each side of the cube and then laminate it, if desired. (You can pick one question from each level for each side of the cube: one knowledge question, one comprehension, and so forth.)
3. Cut out each cube, fold along the dotted lines, and secure the edges with tape.
4. Give a cube to a student or group of students. Each takes a turn rolling the cube. If the first roll turns up a task the student doesn't want to do, he is allowed a second roll. As students work on their own tasks, they also can help each other.
5. When the tasks are complete, have students form groups with those who did the same task on the cube. Allow them time to share their products with one another.

GR: 4–6

Learning modality:
Visual, auditory, kinesthetic, tactile

Group size: Whole group, small group, individual

VARIATIONS

- Tier this activity by making cubes of two different colors. For example, if you have a yellow cube and a green cube, the students using the yellow cube questions might be at or below their grade level

►ASSESSMENT◄

in reading ability. Those using the green cubes might be at or above their grade level. Students who do yellow cube activities will need to do some green cube activities later, working in small groups or directly with you.

• Make large-sized cubes (Kleenex boxes covered with construction paper work well) and attach a library pocket to each side to hold the questions/statements.

• You can put more than one question or statement in each pocket and let students choose which to do.

►ASSESSMENT◄

Off to See the Wizard

Introduction

This can serve as a review/check-up for individual students or as a whole-class activity.

Materials

- Sheets of yellow paper
- Markers
- Wizard face (see reproducible, page 129)

Directions

1. Draw 10 to 12 "bricks," each approximately 3 by 6 inches, on the sheets of paper, laminate each sheet, and cut the bricks apart.
2. If used for individual review/check-up, place a number of yellow bricks on the floor with a different concept printed on each. For example, if checking a kindergartner's knowledge of letter sounds, write a letter on each brick and ask the child to produce or identify the sound.
3. Place one brick after another on the floor, leading to the Wizard.
4. Ask the child to start at the first brick, identify the sound, and then step onto that brick. Have him do the same with the next brick and the next, seeing how many he can identify and how close he can get to the Wizard.
5. For a whole-group activity, attach blank yellow bricks to the bulletin board so they are heading toward the Wizard. Write the name of a state, for example, on each brick and ask the students to name its capital.

GR: K–3

Learning modality: Visual, kinesthetic

Group size: Whole group, individual

VARIATION

- As the class masters a concept or standard for their grade, write it on a yellow brick. The goal is to reach the Wizard by a designated time.

► ASSESSMENT ◄

Mystery Box

Introduction

Use this strategy to determine what students already know or think they know about a topic.

Materials

- Shoebox or paper bag
- Small objects, photographs, or words related to a single unit of study

Directions

1. In a box or bag, place several objects, photos, or words connected to a single concept/unit that you will be teaching. For example, if you are beginning to study plant life, you might include a packet of seeds, a small bottle of water, sunglasses, a baggie of dirt, and a small garden tool.
2. Let children remove one item at a time and ask them to identify the item and relate what they know about it.
3. As more items are removed, ask children what the main concept might be.
4. Place all items on a table or tray that remains accessible to the children while the unit is being taught.

VARIATIONS

- If you are beginning to study oceanography, the shoebox could include photographs of objects such as underwater cameras, robots, or submarines.

- If you are beginning a geography unit about a country or region, include photographs of the place that show various aspects of the culture, such as clothing, food, architecture, etc. Students could guess where the place is by observing the clues in the pictures (terrain, types of trees, houses or churches, etc.).

GR: K–6

Learning modality: Visual, kinesthetic, tactile

Group size: Whole group

► ASSESSMENT ◄

Most Difficult First

Introduction

Having students do the most difficult task first recognizes and addresses the needs of gifted students by allowing them to test out of an assignment. This is an example of curriculum compacting—a process in which you establish what the learning objectives are going to be for a particular subject, pretest or assess your students to find out how much they already know about it, and based on their prior mastery, compress (or compact) the volume of work they are required to do.

Directions

1. Explain to students that they will be given the option of testing out of an assignment by doing the most difficult part first.
2. Identify that part and ask the students to complete it. If they reach proficiency, tell them they do not have to do the rest of the assignment.
3. Next, give them options for other work that is engaging and meaningful while the other students finish the assignment.

GR: 1–6

Learning modality:
Visual

Group size: Individual

▶ ASSESSMENT ◀

Great Wall of Learning

Introduction

Children learn differently. Children remember differently. This simple strategy will provide any student with immediate recall when needed.

Materials

- Bulletin board, white board, or chart paper and stand
- 5 index cards per student

Directions

1. Label the board, chart paper, or stand the Learning Wall.
2. Distribute index cards to the students.
3. Explain to them that any time during a class period (upper grade students) or during the day (primary classes) that they have an "aha" moment, or when a new learning fact is vital to them, they need to write that fact on their index card and place it on the Learning Wall.
4. Allow students to visit the wall any time during the class, even during tests or reviews.

VARIATION

- Usually an "aha" moment happens when students make a connection between new information and previous knowledge, so ask them to explain how the "aha" moment came into their minds.

GR: 2–5

Learning modality:
Visual

Group size: Any

► ASSESSMENT ◄

Random Exit

Introduction

This strategy allows teachers to check the understanding of specific students at any given time during a lesson or class.

Materials

- Index cards

Directions

1. Before class or the period begins, decide who needs a check-up that day and write questions on the index cards.
2. As students enter the room, appear to randomly distribute the index cards, making sure you give the students you're assessing the card you intended.
3. Direct those students to write their answers to the questions on their cards and then ask a neighbor to check their answers.
4. Explain that the cards must be turned in before the students can be dismissed. Make sure the students sign their cards and that the neighbors who checked them sign as well.

VARIATION

- Instead of exit cards, use them as homework passes.

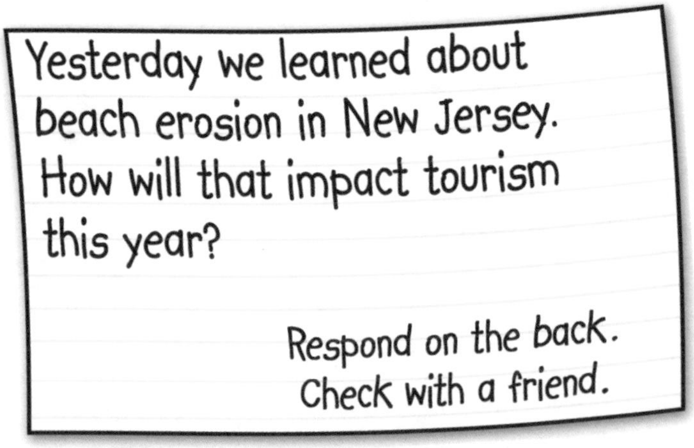

GR: 2–6

Learning modality: Visual

Group size: Individual

Yesterday we learned about beach erosion in New Jersey. How will that impact tourism this year?

Respond on the back.
Check with a friend.

Think-Tac-Toe (Comprehension)

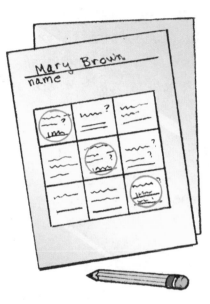

Introduction

Think-Tac-Toes are popular anchor activities in a differentiated classroom. Anchor activities are assignments students can turn to while you are working with others.

Materials

- Think-Tac-Toe sheet, (see reproducible, page 130), one for each student

Directions

1. Give each student a copy of the reproducible.
2. Ask students to choose three activities to complete based on a story they have read and have them indicate to you which ones they chose.
3. Point out to them that the three activities must form a tic-tac-toe vertically, horizontally, or diagonally.

VARIATION

- Rather than giving them a choice, ask students to complete certain activities. For example, you might assign a higher-level student activities #1, #5, and #9 to complete a diagonal tic-tac-toe.

GR: 3–6

Learning modality:
Visual, auditory, kinesthetic, tactile

Group size: Individual

► ASSESSMENT ◄

How Much Is Too Much?

Introduction

Often, when given a timed test, students of all levels struggle with the concept of time. Sometimes 5 minutes can seem like an hour to a young child and other times 5 minutes is never enough for an older student. Since all learners are now expected to conform to time restrictions during state and local testing, it is imperative that classroom teachers help learners conceptualize time frames.

Materials

- Recording sheet
- Stopwatch or wristwatch with a second hand
- Material for covering the classroom clock

Directions

1. Make a recording sheet that includes each student's name and two columns next to the name, where times will be recorded by a student assigned to be "watcher/recorder."

2. Cover the class clock so students cannot see the time.

3. Have students write the numbers 1 through 10 on a piece of paper.

4. Provide the watcher/recorder with a copy of the recording sheet.

5. Give the students a simple task, such as reading three pages in their book. Tell them that once they have finished, they are to signal the watcher/recorder, who will record the elapsed time on the recording sheet. They also are to write on their paper next to #1 how long they think it took them.

6. Next, assign them another task, such as cleaning out their desks. When they've finished, or you direct them to stop, ask them to again signal the watcher/recorder, guestimate how long the task took, and write the guess next to #2 on their paper.

GR: 3–5

Learning modality:
Visual, auditory, kinesthetic, tactile

Group size: Whole group, small group

► ASSESSMENT ◄

7. Now, have students check their guesses against their actual time, which was recorded by the watcher/recorder.

8. Repeat this throughout a day or a week so students will learn how to pace themselves accordingly. By giving them a greater awareness of the amount of time that passes during various tasks, students can learn to estimate the time they will need for future work.

►ASSESSMENT◄

What's the Answer?

Introduction

In this day of high-stakes testing, students must be familiar with a variety of test responses. This activity provides good practice for listening comprehension.

Materials

- 5–10 index cards per student

Directions

1. Distribute index cards to each student. The age and need of the student will determine how many cards each should have, but to begin with, give each one two cards.
2. Ask the students to write at the top of one card "true" and at the top of the second card "false."
3. Make a statement, such as "Halloween is in November," and ask the students to hold up the card with their answer.
4. Next, give the students four cards each and ask them to label one with "A," another with "B," another with "C," and the last with "D." Read a brief text, or project the text on an overhead, and have them read along with you. Ask them multiple-choice questions based on the text and have them answer by holding up the card with their answer.

GR: 3–6

Learning modality:
Visual, auditory, kinesthetic

Group size: Whole group

TIP

- Be careful about the wording of questions, which can be confusing to students, such as "Which of the following is least likely to occur?" or "All of the answers listed below are true except..." Try to make questions as clear as possible.

► ASSESSMENT ◄

Assess Yourself!

Assess Yourself

Name _____

Define the following words:	My Guess Date _____	Actual Meaning Date _____	How is your guess different from your final answer?
1. vanish	argue	to disappear	a lot different
2. cautious	careful	to be careful	got this one!
3.			
4.			
5.			
6.			
7.			
8.			

Categorize	Categorize	Categorize	Make a Prediction: What will the text be about?
Start with "c" 1. curious	1.	1.	I think it will be about some people who get lost
2. cautious	2.	2.	
3. caring	3.	3	

Introduction

This is a before-, during-, and after-reading vocabulary strategy. It will help your students activate prior knowledge, make predictions, and categorize. It is also a great way for students to participate in the assessment process as they will be highlighting, keeping track of, and monitoring their own vocabulary learning. In a differentiated classroom, students are involved in the assessment process.

Materials

- Assess Yourself sheet (see reproducible, page 131), one for each student

Directions

1. Before Reading:
   a. Choose important words from the text students are about to read and list them in the first column of the reproducible.
   b. Give students each a copy of the reproducible. Ask them to individually read the words, guess their meanings, and write their guesses in the second column.
   c. In pairs, have students try to categorize the words and make a prediction about the text.
2. During Reading: Collect the Assess Yourself sheets. Point out to students that as they read, they will encounter the words that were listed on the reproducible.
3. After Reading:
   a. Give the Assess Yourself sheets back to students.
   b. Ask students to fill out the third column with the actual meaning of the word.
   c. Finally, in the fourth column, have students reflect on the difference between their first guess and their final answer.

GR: 2–6

Learning modality: Visual, auditory

Group size: Pairs/triad, individual

► MANAGEMENT ◄

Slap Me Five

Introduction

This is a simple way for students to show their appreciation for you and to help you create a caring atmosphere in your classroom. Teachers have reported that this also appeals to students when their teacher is absent or unavailable.

Materials
- Transparency of your hand

Directions
1. Photocopy your hand and make a transparency of it.
2. Make a paper copy of the reverse side of the transparency (this makes your hand come out correctly).
3. Laminate the hand and attach it to the wall next to your classroom door.
4. Invite students to "slap me five" as they pass by your hand, if they would like to.

GR: K–6

Learning modality:
Visual, kinesthetic, tactile

Group size: Individual

►MANAGEMENT◄

Question Chips

Introduction

Some children interrupt repeatedly and ask "simple questions" that they could figure out for themselves. Resolve this interruption by using Question Chips.

Materials

- Play money or bingo chips
- Coin purse or resealable plastic bag, one per child

Directions

1. Place the coins or chips inside the purse or plastic bag and give one to each child. (The number of coins/chips included will depend on the needs of each child, but don't forget to reduce the number as time goes by.)

2. Explain to the children that they each get to ask you a certain number of questions each day, but that each question asked will cost them a coin/chip. Point out the difference between questions that are good and those that are "wasted," and let them know that they have the option of asking their classmates questions (which won't cost anything) instead of you. (Using other students as teachers reinforces the information/lesson in the minds of the "student teacher," too.)

3. Tell your students that when they have used up all their coins/chips, they can't ask you any more questions for that day.

GR: K–1

Learning modality:
Visual, kinesthetic, tactile

Group size: Individual

TIP

- Instead of coins or bingo chips, use carnival/movie tickets.

► MANAGEMENT ◄

Book of Experts

Introduction

Many small things can eat away at instruction time and interrupt your pace throughout the day, such as a child's request to tie his shoe or to help him find a word. To remedy this, create a Book of Experts, which will allow children to become more independent of you. Find "jobs" within the class that some children can perform at an acceptable level and let them be the experts.

Materials

- Construction paper
- Photos of children (optional)

Directions

1. Make a Book of Experts, using construction paper as the front and back covers and plain sheets of paper for the book pages.
2. Write "Book of Experts" on the front cover and "JOB" at the top of each page.
3. With help from the children, come up with a job that some of the children are able to do, such as tying shoes, and write the heading "Tie Shoes" underneath JOB.
4. Ask the children to raise their hands if they know how to tie their shoes, and then have those children perform the skill, so you can be sure they really know how to do it.
5. Write their names on that page and consider putting a picture of the child next to his name to help young children identify the experts.
6. Continue in the same fashion with other jobs, such as Read Directions, etc.
7. Once you've covered an adequate number of jobs (you can always add more), put the book in an accessible place so that the children can refer to it when they need something done, instead of coming to you first.

GR: K–3

Learning modality:
Visual, kinesthetic

Group size: Individual

►MANAGEMENT◄

VARIATION

- This works well with older students, too. Instead of making a book, however, just keep a list of names of students who perform certain tasks well. When a student, for example, needs a math procedure explained, send him to a student who knows how to do the task.

TIP

- Make sure that the jobs listed include skills that every student can feel comfortable with. Each student should have at least a couple of jobs that she is capable of doing so she doesn't feel left out. Also, try not to have the talented students' names on every page so that those who are less talented won't feel inadequate.

►MANAGEMENT◄

How Are You Doing?

Introduction

Management is key to the success of a differentiated classroom. When students, working independently or in small groups, can signal how they are doing from their seats instead of waiting in line, they spend more time on task and minimize teacher interruptions.

Materials

- Green, yellow, and red paper or plastic cups (small size)

Directions:

1. Give each student three cups—one of each color.
2. When students are working independently, as partners, or in small groups, explain that they can signal to you how they are doing by stacking their cups in a particular order.
3. Tell them that if they are "doing fine," they put the green cup on top of the stack. If they want you to stop by and reassure them that they are on the right track, they put the yellow cup on top. If the red cup is on top, they are signaling that they can't go on without you: "Please help!"

VARIATION

- Keep three different color cups on your desk and use them for noise control. For example, green could mean "group-work voices;" yellow, "whisper voices;" and red, "silent."

GR: K–6

Learning modality:
Visual, kinesthetic

Group size: Whole group, small group, pair/triad, individual

►MANAGEMENT◄

Orchestra Seating

Introduction

Have you noticed that the students in the front of the floor area where you do group work are always the same ones? They are the organized kids, who get there first every time. Here's a way to even things out and ensure that each student has an opportunity to be closest to the lesson and to you.

Materials

• Rolls of different color tape

Directions

1. Using the tape, put multiple colored lines on the floor area where your class meets for large-group activities or lessons. Make sure each line is a different color so each can be easily identified. For example, the green line could be first, then red, purple, orange, and blue.

2. When reading aloud and showing pictures, the students on the green line will have the best advantage of seeing and hearing, so have the kids move back one line each day. If a student was on the green line yesterday, he will be on the red line today; if a student was on the blue line yesterday, she will be right up front on the green one today.

VARIATION

• If you prefer to sit in a large circle, use pieces of tape to show the space where each student sits. Students then move around the circle, clockwise or counterclockwise, from one piece of tape to the next.

GR: K–3

Learning modality:
Visual, auditory, kinesthetic

Group size: Whole group

Ten Tips for Motivation

Introduction

Motivation, praise, and recognition are key elements in any classroom, but they are particularly important in a differentiated classroom. You want students to work together and accept one another's uniqueness and differences. You model that behavior for them by your words and actions.

Directions

1. Find out what students can do and then ask them to do a little more. In a differentiated classroom, the level of an assignment should push students a little beyond what they can do. Support them as you challenge them.

2. It is important not to get side-tracked by arguing about or debating the validity of a student's excuse. A better practice is to ignore the excuse and attack the problem by focusing on the student's work. For example, when a student tells you that he would have finished but other students kept interrupting, say, "What is the status of your work now and when will you be finished?" The right answer keeps the discussion focused on the work and not on the excuse.

3. Avoid the word "but" in your dealings with your students. Any time you use the word "but," what you are really saying is that you disagree with the student. For example, if you say, "I agree with you, but let me tell you this…," students will wonder if you really do agree with them. The solution is to replace the word "but" with the word "and." So you would say, "I agree with you, and let me tell you this…" This way you will eliminate all contradictions from your message and your words will be more influential and motivating.

4. Motivate by praising behavior as well as by defining it. For example, say, "Thank you for picking up the scraps. You really helped us out."

GR: K–6

Learning modality:
Visual, auditory

Group size: Any

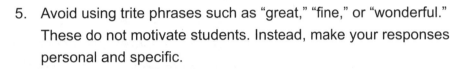

▶ MANAGEMENT ◀

5. Avoid using trite phrases such as "great," "fine," or "wonderful." These do not motivate students. Instead, make your responses personal and specific.

6. Some students, especially those with a negative reputation, are motivated by private praise. They want to avoid competition, embarrassment, or the "teacher's pet" label.

7. Motivation is enhanced when you draw attention to student effort. Say, "You learned your facts with such accuracy. You must have spent a lot of time practicing."

8. Teacher-pleasing phrases such as, "I am so proud of you!" or "I really like the way you…" do not motivate. Turn the attention back to the student by saying, "You should feel proud," or "Good for you!"

9. Comparing students does not motivate.

10. Teach students how to show appreciation for one another. This requires time working with students to help them feel self-confident so that they can be secure enough within themselves to recognize positives in their classmates. Role-modeling is a great activity to help with this.

►MANAGEMENT◄

Quick Card Count

Introduction

This is a quick way to survey the classroom for lunch count, responses to content questions, and classroom choices. It's also a hands-on approach to graphing.

Materials

- Magnetic business cards (available from office supply stores), one for each student

Directions

1. Give students each a magnetic business card and let them decorate theirs as they wish.

2. Write a question on the blackboard or white board so that there are three choices for answering it, and put each possible answer at the top of one of three columns. Examples are as follows:

> After reading Chapter 3 in today's story, who believes that:
> > *Michael was right.   Mrs. Jones was right.   I have no opinion.*
> > **OR**
> When traveling to the Gold Rush, which of the following means of transportation would you have preferred and why?
> > *covered wagon   open wagon   lone horse*
> > **OR**
> If you could have one of the following amounts of money, which would you prefer and why?
> > *1,000 pennies   50 quarters $10 bill*

3. Ask the students to come forward and place their business card in the column that gives their answer.

TIP

- Tape a business card to the front of a fish bowl, empty coffee can, or some other container where students' cards can be stored.

GR: K–6

Learning modality:
Visual, kinesthetic

Group size: Whole group

►MANAGEMENT◄

Read the Walls

MORNING PROCEDURE

1. Empty your backpack.
2. Put your clothespin next to your lunch choice.
3. Put your homework in the red basket.
4. Sharpen two pencils.
5. Say "hello" to a classmate.
6. Read a book or write in your journal.
7. Have a great day!

GR: K–4

Learning modality:
Visual, auditory, kinesthetic, tactile

Group size: Any

Introduction

The management of a differentiated classroom is often a challenge, but your classroom walls can help you. The following strategy suggests ways to use your walls for procedures and interactive learning. When students know the routine, it makes it much easier to have different students involved in different activities.

Directions

1. On a wall or on your interactive bulletin board, post a procedure you want your students to follow.
2. Model each step of the procedure for the students: you do a step and then ask them to do it; you do the next step, and then they do it.
3. Repeat, if necessary, until you are confident that all students know the routine.

Note: For K–1 students, you will need to include picture clues.

VARIATION

• For an open house, assign students to explain procedures and interactive bulletin boards to parents.

Bulletin Boards

• **Graffitti Board:** Promotes student inquiry through various sentence stems and students' written responses to books. Sentence stems could include: "When I read…," "I liked…," "I wonder…," "My favorite part was…"

• **Theme Board:** List vocabulary words by themes such as feeling words, cold words, words other than "said," etc. or focus on current instructional themes in social studies and/or science. You might include key questions, research information, etc.

• **Menu Boards:** Contains a menu of activities from which students choose different activities from a specific content area.

►MANAGEMENT◄

Be Here Now

Introduction

A growing number of students experience difficulty focusing and paying attention, which negatively impacts academic performance. The following tools and techniques can assist students in dealing with these issues and increase their learning time.

Materials

- Remote control for overhead (see Note below)
- Various types of pointers
- Colored acetate or highlighting tape
- Sticky arrows

Directions

1. When moving around the room between the overhead and the word wall, for example, use the remote control to turn the overhead off and on. Otherwise, ADD students may still be focused on the overhead when you want their attention instead on the word wall.
   Note: In order to operate the overhead with a remote control device, you will need a wireless AC outlet control (available at electronic equipment stores). Plug it into the wall outlet and then plug the overhead projector into the outlet control.
2. If explaining something on the overhead, lay a pointer on the exact place that you are referring to so all students can stay on target.
3. Use strips of colored acetate or highlighting tape to mark where you want students to focus.
4. Apply a sticky arrow to a page of text where there's something specific you want students to see—a caption under a graphic or a specific topic sentence in a paragraph.

GR: K–6

Learning modality:
Visual, auditory, kinesthetic

Group size: Whole group, small group, individual

►MANAGEMENT◄

TIPS

- Use "first-class" seating with your ADD students. When these students sit in the back of the room, they see what all the kids between them and you are doing. When they are up front, they can see the board and hear better. Plus, you are right there and can point to where you want them to focus.

- Cut down on distractions by allowing students to wear noise-suppressing head phones while reading or working on an assignment.

- Instead of colored acetate, use transparent colored plastic folders and cut them into strips.

►MANAGEMENT◄

The "Frugal Teacher" Desk Carrel

Introduction

Here's a quick, inexpensive alternative to a commercial carrel. It is a handy way to provide a little privacy for students who are easily distracted or overly concerned that others are looking at their work. This can be student- or teacher-initiated.

Materials

- Manila file folders or sheets of paper

Directions

1. Tape two file folders together along their tab edges and stand them up on end to create a privacy screen.
2. Or, fold a sheet of paper in half crosswise like a book, open it up, and lay it flat, landscape style. From the bottom, fold up about a quarter of the page, so that it looks like a pocket portfolio (see illustration). Lay it flat again and cut or tear the sheet along the middle (vertical) fold line and up to the lengthwise (horizontal) fold line (see illustration). Stand it up along the bottom, lengthwise fold and overlap the bottom edges, forming a screen.
3. Allow students to use these when they wish.

GR: K–6

Learning modality:
Visual, auditory

Group size: Individual

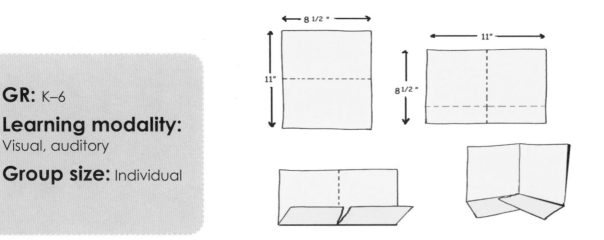

►MANAGEMENT◄

Thought Is Taught

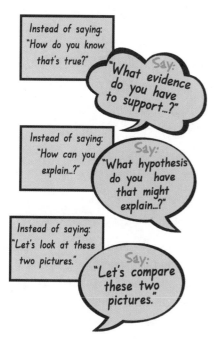

Introduction

One of the goals in a differentiated classroom is to equip all students with thinking skills. Today's teacher must prepare students for jobs and technologies not yet created, which is different from the classroom of the past in which you could give your students skills and knowledge that you had found useful. In order to prepare students for the challenges of the 21st century, you must find ways to "draw information out" and not "stuff information into" your students. Student thinking must be deliberately taught.

Materials

- Thought Is Taught sheet (see reproducible, page 132)

Directions

1. Make a copy of the reproducible and keep it close at hand.
2. Refer to it throughout the day to guide your classroom instruction so that you are encouraging and extending the thinking of your students.
3. Remind yourself to use thinking words in your own questioning vocabulary.

TIP

- Laminate your copy of the reproducible so it will last longer and will not be easily misplaced.

GR: K–6

Learning modality:
Visual, auditory

Group size: Whole group

►MANAGEMENT◄

Differentiating with the Overactive Student in Mind

Introduction

Differentiating the classroom environment, while keeping the needs of overactive students in mind, will create a positive, caring atmosphere conducive to learning. A noticeable reduction in classroom disruptions and distractions will be evident immediately.

Materials

- Differentiating with the Overactive Student in Mind (see reproducible, page 133)
- Desk/chair casters, tennis balls, Wikki Stix, desk carrels, fidget box, noise-suppressing headset, remote control device, sand-filled draft stopper, clay, stress ball, Play-Doh, noodle flotation device, felt, rubber bungee cord, ball chair, weighted vest, and pillow

Directions

1. Keep a copy of the reproducible at hand and, working closely with special education personnel, tailor the strategies and accommodations according to your students' needs.
2. Notify parents of any adaptations/accommodations you will be making.

TIP

- Allow all students to use these materials when/if desired, so those who really need such accommodations don't stand out from the other students.

GR: K–6

Learning modality:
Visual, auditory, kinesthetic

Group size: Individual

►MANAGEMENT◄

Bubble Gum Groups

Introduction

Try this fun method of random grouping. Just be sure to check your school's policy first regarding the use of gum and candy in the classroom.

Materials

- Gumball machine (available from toy stores)
- Gumballs
- Pennies, if needed, for the machine

Directions

1. Give students each a turn at the gumball machine.
2. Tell them to form teams—or to find seat partners or reading partners—by joining those students whose gumballs are the same color as theirs.
3. Once everyone has found their partners/teammates, proceed with your group work.

VARIATION

- Use the gumball machine for rewards. For example, if a student correctly completes three problems, he turns the knob and gets a treat.

GR: K–6

Learning modality:
Visual, kinesthetic

Group size: Whole group

►MANAGEMENT◄

CD Cut-Ups

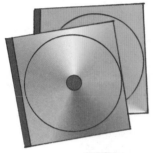

Introduction

Using music that is popular with preteens and teens is an effective and engaging way to get students into smaller groups. In addition, it shows students that you are interested in learning more about them and allows them to get to know each other better as well.

Materials

- Index cards

Directions

1. Go to a local music store and ask one of the clerks to direct you to the area of top preteen and teen music CDs.
2. Select five to six CDs, examine the single song titles, and write down the name of each CD plus four to five selections from each one.
   Note: Be careful about your selections since popular music today oftentimes includes language and hidden meanings you would not want to encourage or seem to be promoting.
3. Write the individual song titles on the index cards, one title per card.
4. Give one card to each student as he enters class and tell him to join the students who have the titles that are from the same CD.
5. After students are in their groups, ask them to explain why their group goes together and to identify the recording artist of their CD.

VARIATIONS

- Use this same technique with picture books, movie titles, or titles of novels (writing characters' names from the book, movie, or novel onto individual index cards).

- Use the names of college or professional sports teams.

TIP

- Be sure to keep a "cheat sheet" at hand so you can check the way your students have grouped themselves.

GR: 2–6

Learning modality:
Visual, auditory, kinesthetic, tactile

Group size: Whole group

► **MANAGEMENT** ◄

Got Homework?

Introduction

Many students experience organizational problems. Doing homework and then misplacing it is a good example. This technique will help those students keep a running record of what they've done and where it is.

Materials

- Homework Recording Sheet (see reproducible, page 134)
- 9 x 12-inch manila envelopes

Directions

1. Make copies of the reproducible and distribute to the students. If you teach more than one subject in your class, give students a copy for each subject. Do the same with the envelopes.
2. Have students tape the envelope to the inside back cover of their notebooks, and then tape the recording sheet to the envelope (see illustration).
3. Tell students to record each assignment on their sheets, showing the date assigned and the date due. As they complete each assignment, they place it inside the envelope.
4. Make an agreement with students that if they claim they did their homework, then it should be in their assignment envelope.

GR: 3–6

Learning modality: Visual

Group size: Individual

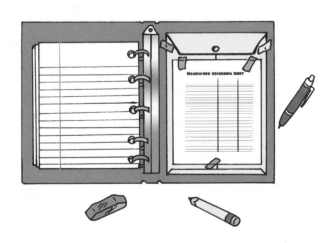

►MANAGEMENT◄

USA (Unique Skills and Activities)

Introduction

In a differentiated classroom, students need options for times when they finish early or they are stuck and don't know what to do. This versatile sponge activity enables you to use the same questions every day but to apply them to the current day's newspaper, so that the answers change each day. Using newspapers enables students to work with relevant and real information and details. It also keeps them actively engaged and on task.

Materials

* Newspaper of your choice

Directions

1. Point out to your students where you have posted questions from various subject categories—math, social studies, reading, etc.
2. Tell them that when they finish an assignment early, they have to work on something else, and that this sponge activity is a good option. They have the added bonus of being able to decide what subject to choose.
3. Model this before your students do it on their own. An example might be as follows:
   a. If the student chooses social studies, he takes the newspaper and reads the tasks that are posted for this subject. In this example, he is asked to find a weather map, locate a city on the map closest to where he is, and then find what the day's highs and lows will be in that city.
   b. He also is asked to figure the difference between the temperatures.
   c. Next, he is to locate the city with the highest temperature and the city with the lowest, and then figure the difference between them.

GR: 3–6

Learning modality:
Visual, auditory, kinesthetic, tactile

Group size: Individual

▶MANAGEMENT◀

4. These tasks remain posted on the board, but the next day, the answers will be different because the information in that day's newspaper will have changed.

VARIATIONS

- For practice reading a table, ask the student to turn to the TV section and identify programs that last exactly one hour.

- For practice with place value, ask the student to turn to the financial or sports section and identify whole numbers or decimals, using different colored highlighters.

- For math practice, ask the student to turn to the sports section and create an organized list of the ways particular football scores could have been made.

- For language arts practice, have students highlight two-syllable nouns, verbs, etc.

- For reading practice, take articles from the story section, cut off the headlines, cut apart the articles, mix everything up, and have students piece the articles back together.

►TEACHING TOOLS◄

Word Stretcher

Introduction

This tool adds visual, kinesthetic, and tactile dimensions to sounding out words—and provides a great way to embrace multiple learning modalities in one activity.

Materials

- 1-inch-wide sewing elastic
- Needle and thread
- One-hole punch
- Hook parts from hook and eyes
- Index cards

Directions

1. Take a piece of sewing elastic and sew the hooks along the edge of one side, spacing the hooks so that they are a little more than 3 inches apart (see illustration). The length of the sewing elastic will be determined by the length of the words you want to make.

2. Punch a hole in the middle of one of the short ends of each index card and write a letter on each card (see illustration).

3. Select a word you want your students to practice, such as "cat." Hang the index cards with the letters "c," "a," and "t" from the hooks on the sewing elastic so that they spell the word "cat" (see illustration).

GR: K–1

Learning modality:
Visual, auditory, kinesthetic, tactile

Group size: Pair/triad, individual

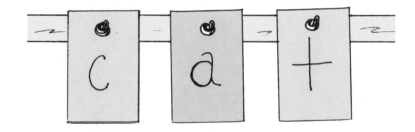

►TEACHING TOOLS◄

4. Hold up both ends of the elastic so your students can see the word "cat," and ask them to sound out the word as you pull on the elastic, stretching the letters apart.

5. Now ask the students to put the sounds together as the elastic is relaxed and the letters come back together again.

6. Allow students time to practice with the Word Stretcher. Then change the first letter in the word to something else, such as "h" and repeat the steps for the word "hat."

TIPS

• Use business cards instead of index cards, but decrease the spacing between the hooks.

• Make a number of Word Stretchers so you have plenty to go around.

• Take precautions to avoid eye injuries; tell students to always hold the elastic at waist or stomach level when using the Word Stretchers.

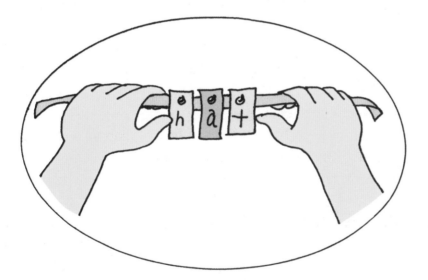

►TEACHING TOOLS◄

Raised Lines

Introduction

Raised lines provide a hands-on way for students to stay within the lines and margins when writing, thus creating a pathway to success.

Materials

- Serrated tracing wheel (available at fabric or art supply stores and from Crystal Springs Books, see Resources, pages 107–108)
- Ruler
- Sheets of unlined paper

Directions

1. Place a sheet of paper on top of a magazine or a few layers of newspaper. Using the tracing wheel, roll it along the edge of the ruler, marking a writing line across the paper. Make as many or as few lines on each sheet as is appropriate for your students.
   Note: Be sure to do this on the *back* side of the paper so the lines are raised on the front side, where the students can feel them.
2. Once you have a supply of these pages ready, pass them out to those students who need them, but if others are interested, supply them with sheets as well.
3. Ask students to feel the lines on their papers and to notice how their pen/pencil "bumps" into the lines as they write.
4. Allow time for students to practice on their sheets.

VARIATIONS

- Use raised lines to mark the left and right margins on the sheet as well for those students who need a reminder of where to begin and where to stop writing.

- Use raised lines to mark the fold lines when making three-dimensional forms like cubes.

TIP

- Be sure the paper is placed on a soft surface because the tracing wheel will not mark as well on a hard one.

GR: K–1

Learning modality:
Visual, auditory, tactile

Group size: Individual

►TEACHING TOOLS ◄

Card Holders for Little Hands

Introduction

This is an ideal way for little hands to hold onto and keep track of a number of cards at once. It also is beneficial to those who have not developed fine motor skills.

Materials

- Margarine lids
- Brass fasteners
- Playing cards

Directions

1. Place two same-size lids together, front to front, so that their rims are on the outside.
2. Push a brass fastener through the middle of both and tighten.
3. Insert playing cards between the two lids on the top half. Little hands can hold the bottom.

TIP

- If the cards are small, use clear lids so the child can see the entire card when it is placed in the holder.

GR: K–2

Learning modality:
Kinesthetic, tactile

Group size: Individual

►TEACHING TOOLS◄

Popcorn Word Bottles

Introduction

This activity is sure to get the attention of those hard-to-focus kids in your class.

Materials

- Light-weight copy paper in neon or bright colors
- ½ cup popcorn kernels
- 2-liter clear soda bottle, label removed
- Piece of wool (optional)

Directions

1. Cut colored copy paper into strips, each measuring approximately 1½ x 3 inches.
2. Write a "popcorn" word (high-frequency words that keep "popping up") on both sides of the strips of paper, using black ink.
3. Pour the popcorn kernels into the soda bottle.
4. Carefully insert five or so of the popcorn words through the top of the bottle, being careful not to crease the paper strips.
5. Rub the bottle against the back of your head or with a piece of wool cloth to create static electricity.
6. Pass the bottle around and let the kids take turns reading the words that are sticking to its sides.

VARIATION

- Let students make their own Popcorn Word Bottles to study weekly spelling words that are challenging.

GR: K–3

Learning modality: Visual, kinesthetic

Group size: Whole group, small group, individual

►TEACHING TOOLS ◄

The Crowning Touch

Introduction

Create crowns to represent circular concepts such as days of the week; months of the year; life cycles of a pumpkin, frog, or butterfly; and so forth.

Materials

• Sentence strips

Directions

1. On a sentence strip, write a circular concept (life cycle) or a song ("Row, Row, Row Your Boat") that has a repetitive theme.
2. Attach both ends of the strip, creating a crown, to show how the beginning starts over again once you get to the end.
3. Let children take turns wearing the crown each time you do the activity.

GR: K–3

Learning modality:
Visual, kinesthetic

Group size: Whole group, small group, individual

►TEACHING TOOLS◄

Leveling the Playing Field

Introduction

Any time games are used in a classroom, all children should be able to play and gain some level of information. Be sure to create or choose games that allow everyone to participate at his or her own level.

Materials

* Index cards

Directions

1. Create a set of flash cards from the index cards to represent a concept, such as letters. The cards should have the letter written in a basic color, a picture clue of a word that starts with that letter, and the word underneath that.

2. Have children pick cards and say anything they "know" about the card. A child may say, "I see green." The teacher may reply, "It is a green letter B. B is at the beginning of "bear" and /b/ makes this sound." So, the basic answer of green can lead to higher-level concepts such as letter identification, oral language (labeling), and sounds associated with the letter.

VARIATIONS

* Use shape cards that have colored shapes along with a picture clue of something that is that shape.

* Boost language skills with the Language-Building Box (see Resources, pages 107–108), which uses word cards and picture cards for games and activities.

* Play games with the various ways numbers can be represented to help students develop number sense (see Resources, Number Match Games, pages 107–108). Games are easily differentiated.

GR: K–3

Learning modality: Visual, auditory

Group size: Whole group, small group

► TEACHING TOOLS ◄

Memorable Venn Diagrams

Introduction

Many teachers use graphic organizers, such as Venn diagrams, in the differentiated classroom. To make the lesson all the more appealing, demonstrate with Hoola Hoops.

Materials

- 2 Hoola Hoops
- Sticky notes or small note tablet
- Pens or markers

Directions

1. Draw an example of a Venn diagram on the chalkboard or white board, and explain to your students what it is and how it is used.
2. Next, place the two Hoola Hoops on the floor so that they overlap one another. Label one hoop "apples" and the other "oranges."
3. Ask your students to make statements that describe apples, such as "they are fruits;" "they are red (or yellow, or green) in color;" "they are sweet-tasting;" "they are used in pies;" etc. Write each description on a separate sticky note and have students place each one inside the apples hoop. Do the same with the oranges hoop.
4. Where the two hoops overlap, ask students to place notes that describe what the two fruits have in common: they are fruits, they have seeds, they are sweet-tasting, they are packed in lunches, etc.

GR: 1–6

Learning modality:
Visual, kinesthetic, tactile

Group size: Whole group, small group

►TEACHING TOOLS◄

Can't Go Wrong

Introduction

Using Velcro tape to create game boards allows a teacher to ensure correct placement of important pieces and helps children succeed.

Materials

• Velcro tape

Directions

1. Create a rhyme board where a child must identify the word family and then add to the board those words that are in that word family.
2. To ensure that the children can't go wrong, reverse the Velcro on the board so that only the correct word-family words will stick. For example, "sing" and "bring" are in the "ing" word family so they will have pieces of Velcro on back that will stick to the Velcro on the board.
3. "Song" and "long" do not belong to the "ing" word family, so those words will have Velcro attached that will not stick to the board.

VARIATIONS

• Use this activity with lessons about long and short vowels.

• At the 5th- and 6th-grade levels, use this with spelling and grammar rules.

GR: K–6

Learning modality:
Visual, kinesthetic, tactile

Group size: Whole group, small group, individual

▶TEACHING TOOLS ◀

Recipe Cards for Success

Introduction

To complete an activity, many children need to hear the directions more than once. To eliminate the often repeated question "What do I do?," create recipe cards for your students.

Materials
• 8½ x 11-inch sheets of paper

Directions

1. Turn the paper landscape-style and draw the outline of a large index card.
2. Inside the boxed area, print the name of the activity at the top of the card: Recipe for _____
3. Under that, print the list of materials that are needed, just as the ingredients would appear on a recipe card.
4. Number and write each step in the order that the child must follow to complete the activity.
5. For younger children, add a picture, if there is a final product, at the bottom of the card to show what it "should" look like.

VARIATION
• This activity can also be done with the whole class; write the instructions on an easel and have the students copy what you write.

GR: K–6
Learning modality:
Visual
Group size: Any

►TEACHING TOOLS ◄

Puzzle Facts

Introduction

This activity will help students put information together by visualizing how the pieces fit together. They take the "parts" of information and form the "whole" picture.

Materials

- Marker
- Oak tag
- Pictures or statements of facts from a unit of study

Directions

1. Draw a puzzle on the oak tag, showing each interlocking piece, and give it a title. For example, if studying penguins, you might call it Penguin Facts.

2. Place a picture clue or fact statement in each piece of the puzzle. For penguins, you might write one of the following facts on each puzzle piece:

   Penguins breathe air.
   Penguins are birds.
   Penguins lay eggs.
   Penguins are feathered.
   Penguins cannot fly.

3. Have students cut apart the pieces and then put them back together.

VARIATIONS

- Use the name of a state or country as the title and write on each puzzle piece a fact about the state or country.

- Use a scientific concept as the title with the pieces having supporting ideas or theories.

TIP

- To save yourself time, you might want to purchase some blank white puzzles.

GR: 1–6

Learning modality:
Visual, kinesthetic, tactile

Group size: Small group, individual

►TEACHING TOOLS ◄

Correct with Z-Notes

Introduction

Some students are perfectionists and do not like to see any marks made on their papers; others might be placed in harm's way if they brought home papers with errors marked. This strategy allows you to point out to your students what needs to be corrected without actually marking on their papers.

Materials

- Z-Notes in pink and yellow colors as well as clear (transparent sticky notes available from most office supply stores)

Directions

1. Establish a color code for the Z-Notes and post this in a place where all students can refer to it easily. For example, for language arts, a pink Z-Note on a student's paper could mean that there is a spelling or punctuation error; a yellow Z-Note, a grammatical error; and a clear Z-Note, a need for further clarification.
2. Give students their papers with Z-Notes in place and allow them time to figure out what is wrong and how to correct it.
3. When students have finished working on their papers, have them remove the Z-Notes, return them to a designated place (or to you), and give you their corrected papers.

VARIATION

- You can use Z-Notes with just about any subject, including math, science, social studies, and reading.

TIP

- Instead of using Z-Notes, slip the student's paper inside a page protector and mark on the page protector itself, using a nonpermanent marker.

GR: K–6

Learning modality:
Visual, tactile

Group size: Individual

►TEACHING TOOLS◄

Helping Posters

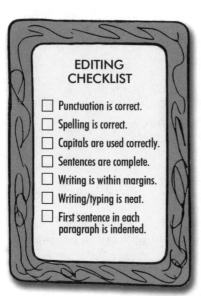

Introduction

Helping posters provide visual support for all students, especially struggling learners. They also encourage students to be independent learners and allow you more uninterrupted time for working with others.

Materials

- Editing Checklist Poster (see reproducible, page 135)
- Asking Words Poster (see reproducible, page 137)
- Capitalization Rules Poster (see reproducible, page 138)
- 6 Division Steps Poster (see reproducible, page 119)
- SQ3R Poster (see reproducible, page 114)
- Hundreds Chart (see reproducible, page 139)

Directions

1. Make enlarged copies of the posters, laminate each one, and hang them around the classroom where they can be easily read by all students, which is generally at eye level.
2. Explain to the students how the posters will support their learning.
3. Point out to students that they should refer to the posters for information before seeking help from you or another classmate.

VARIATIONS

- Create a Color Words poster with hints for remembering to add "colorful" or descriptive words when students are writing.

- Create a Vowel Clues poster, showing, for example, an egg for the short /e/ sound, apple for the short /a/ sound, octopus for the short /o/ sound, and so forth.

TIP

- Some students prefer to have their own personal packet of helping posters, so make copies of the posters on 8½ x 11-inch sheets of paper and have students store them in binders or folders.

GR: 1–6

Learning modality:
Visual

Group size: Whole group, individual

▶TEACHING TOOLS◀

Editing Tools

Introduction

It can be difficult for students to focus on several conventions of print when editing. Provide them with some or all of the following tools and let them discover what works best for them.

Materials

- Editing Tool (see Resources, pages 107–108)
- Whisper/phonics phone (see Resources, pages 107–108)
- Editing Checklist bookmark (see reproducible, page 136)

Directions

Model how each of the tools can be used when editing:

1. With the Editing Tool, for example, demonstrate how the student uses one side at a time, depending on whether she is checking for usage, punctuation, capitalization, or spelling.

2. Encourage students to whisper read using a whisper/phonics phone when editing for correct usage.

3. Provide each student with an Editing Checklist bookmark, as a reminder of what to check.

TIP

- Have students use dry-erase markers on their bookmarks so they can be used repeatedly.

Gr: 2–6

Learning modality:
Visual, auditory, tactile

Group size: Individual

►TEACHING TOOLS◄

Parking Lot

Introduction

Often children will hesitate to raise their hands to ask questions for clarification about topics. This simple accommodation enables students to feel comfortable with sharing their concerns.

Materials

- Large piece of chart or butcher paper
- Packs of sticky notes, any color, size, or shape
- Markers

Directions

1. Label the large piece of paper "Parking Lot" and put it in an easily accessible place in the classroom.
2. Tell your students that any time during the day or class period when they may have a question or concern, they have the privilege of writing it on a sticky note and attaching it to the Parking Lot. For example, if you are teaching a lesson on fractions and Joshua is confused, he can write his name and his issue on a sticky note and place it in the Parking Lot.
3. Monitor the Parking Lot throughout the day, collecting sticky notes and getting back to each student who has posted a note. Talk one-on-one to the student about his question sometime during the day, or discuss the issue with the whole class.

Note: You may need to be flexible the first few times you use this strategy to determine the pacing of answering every student's questions.

TIP

- Tell students to use the hot-pink sticky notes for questions that need an immediate response. Other than those, any color may be used.

Gr: 2–6

Learning modality:
Visual, kinesthetic

Group size: Any

▶TEACHING TOOLS◀

Graphic Artist

Across

1. Very tired
19. What you always ask your teacher
32. Shy
46. Do it _____

Down

1. Opposite of fast
3. Opposite of hard
20. Opposite of cold
34. Not yours but _____

Introduction

Graph paper provides a simple yet effective way to differentiate spelling instruction or any vocabulary review. Students enjoy making their own crossword puzzles.

Materials

- Graph paper (see reproducible, page 140)

Directions

1. Number the spaces on a sheet of graph paper and make a copy for each student (see illustration).
2. Distribute the graph paper and demonstrate how to place vocabulary words in the spaces.
3. After entering a word, the student writes its definition at the bottom of the graph paper.
4. Each word should be written in crossword fashion, horizontally and vertically, using common letters.
5. After checking a student's sheet for accuracy, transfer the definitions to a blank sheet of graph paper and use it as a crossword puzzle for another student. Do the same with the other students' sheets.

VARIATION

- Create a word search (see illustration). First, distribute graph paper and demonstrate how to randomly place spelling words on the paper. Then have students do the same on their graph paper, filling in the blank boxes with random letters. Collect the sheets and have students use their own for review or, as a further challenge, give each student's sheet to someone else.

Word Search

1. Place the following spelling words in boxes: forecast, rain, weather, cloudy
2. Now fill in the blank boxes with any letters.
3. When finished, put your name on the back and turn in.

GR: 3–6

Learning modality:
Visual

Group size: Whole group, small group, individual

▶TEACHING TOOLS ◀

Response Spinner

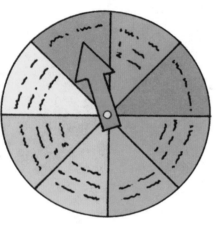

Introduction

This activity encourages a differentiated response to written material in any subject area.

Materials
- Circle and arrow templates (see reproducibles, page 141)
- Oak tag
- Marker
- Brass brad

Directions
1. Trace the circle and the arrow onto oak tag.
2. Laminate and cut out both shapes.
3. Using the marker, divide the circle into equal, pie-shaped sections.
4. Attach the arrow to the center of the circle with a brass brad.
5. Write simple tasks on each section of the circle, such as:
   a. Change the ending of the story and tell it to your group.
   b. List the main characters in the story.
   c. Describe the problem in the story and how you think it should have been solved.
   d. Describe the part of the story you did not like and why.
   e. Change the setting of the story to a location you would prefer and describe the entire story based on the new location.
6. Have students in the group take turns spinning the arrow and responding orally to the topic the arrow lands on.

Gr: 3–6

Learning modality: Visual, auditory, kinesthetic

Group size: Small group

VARIATIONS
- Make a really large circle and arrow from poster board so this can be done with the whole class.
- Turn this into a game show. Assign three students to be judges and split the remainder of the class into two teams. The judges decide on the best responses.
- This can be readily adapted to other content area topics.

► RESOURCES ◄

<u>Related D.I. Products Available Through Crystal Springs Books</u>
10 Sharon Road, PO Box 500
Peterborough, NH 03458
1-800-321-0401
<u>www.crystalsprings.com</u>

Engage ALL Students Through Differentiation by Anne M. Beninghof

Differentiated Instruction: Different Strategies for Different Learners by Char Forsten, Jim Grant, and Betty Hollas

Differentiating Textbooks: Strategies to Improve Student Comprehension & Motivation by Char Forsten, Jim Grant, and Betty Hollas

Differentiating Instruction in a Whole-Group Setting by Betty Hollas

Different Tools for Different Learners: Language Arts Activities to Start Using Today! by Donna VanderWeide

* * * * * * * * * * * *

- Editing Tool
- Finger Pointers
- Highlight Hammer
- Highlighting Tape
- Language-Building Box: Word and Picture Card Games and Activities
- Mini Pigs
- Mini Pointers for Overhead Screen
- *My Writing Words* (K-1, 2-3)
- Number Match Games: Fun ways to play with numbers
- Phonics phone
- Place Value Strips, Disks, and Cubes
- Reading/Writing Tool
- Serrated Tracing Wheel
- Wikki Stix
- Word Whackers

► RESOURCES ◄

* * * * * * * * * * * *

<u>Other Recommended Web Sites</u>

- www.flashcardexchange.com
- www.highlights.com
- www.puzzlemaker.com
- www.reallygoodstuff.com
- www.sde.com
- www.teachernet.com
- www.teachingmadeeasier.com
- www.thesmartiezone.com

Important to Me Words

Dear Parents,

Many children focus on writing about things that are important to them. This means that they have many "Important to Me" words that they want to know how to spell. To assist your child with writing, please help him or her add the words on the attached list to the dictionary included with this letter. Put each word on the correct alphabetical page, underline the first letter of the word if it should be capitalized (e.g., sister's name), and help your child identify the word by making a quick drawing (photos work too) of the person or thing.

Talk with your child about his or her favorite vacation place, family memory, family activity, etc. Brainstorm words that describe the topic.

Please be sure that your child brings the completed dictionary back to class by _____.

Thank you for helping your child become a more independent writer.

Sincerely,

Important to Me Words

Dear Parents,

Many children focus on writing about things that are important to them. This means that they have many "Important to Me" words that they want to know how to spell. To assist your child with writing, please help him or her add the words on the attached list to the dictionary included with this letter. Put each word on the correct alphabetical page, underline the first letter of the word if it should be capitalized (e.g., sister's name), and help your child identify the word by making a quick drawing (photos work too) of the person or thing.

Talk with your child about his or her favorite vacation place, family memory, family activity, etc. Brainstorm words that describe the topic.

Please be sure that your child brings the completed dictionary back to class by _____.

Thank you for helping your child become a more independent writer.

Sincerely,

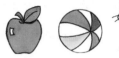

Important to Me Words

Mom's name _____

Dad's name _____

The name your child calls his/her grandparents _____

Siblings' names _____

Pets' names _____

Street you live on _____

Town you live in _____

Favorite color (please write it using that color) _____

Favorite food _____

Favorite show _____

Favorite book _____

Favorite character _____

Favorite toy _____

Please add any other words that you know are "Important to Me" words for your child.

_____

_____

_____

_____

_____

THE MORE WAYS YOU TEACH, THE MORE STUDENTS YOU REACH

Start Your Engines

Word Ladder

THE MORE WAYS YOU TEACH, THE MORE STUDENTS YOU REACH

Personalizing Parts of Speech

Name _____

Noun _____

Pronoun _____

Verb _____

Adjective _____

Adverb _____

Conjunction _____

Preposition _____

Article _____

SQ3R

S   1ˢᵗ   **S**urvey the passage to be read.

Q   2ⁿᵈ   Create **q**uestions from headings and subheadings.

R   3ʳᵈ   **R**ead the passage to answer the questions you have developed.

R   4ᵗʰ   **R**ecite by creating an oral or written summarization of what has been read.

R   5ᵗʰ   **R**eview by answering the questions created for the passage.

Acronym coined by F. P. Robinson, 1946, in his book Effective Study.

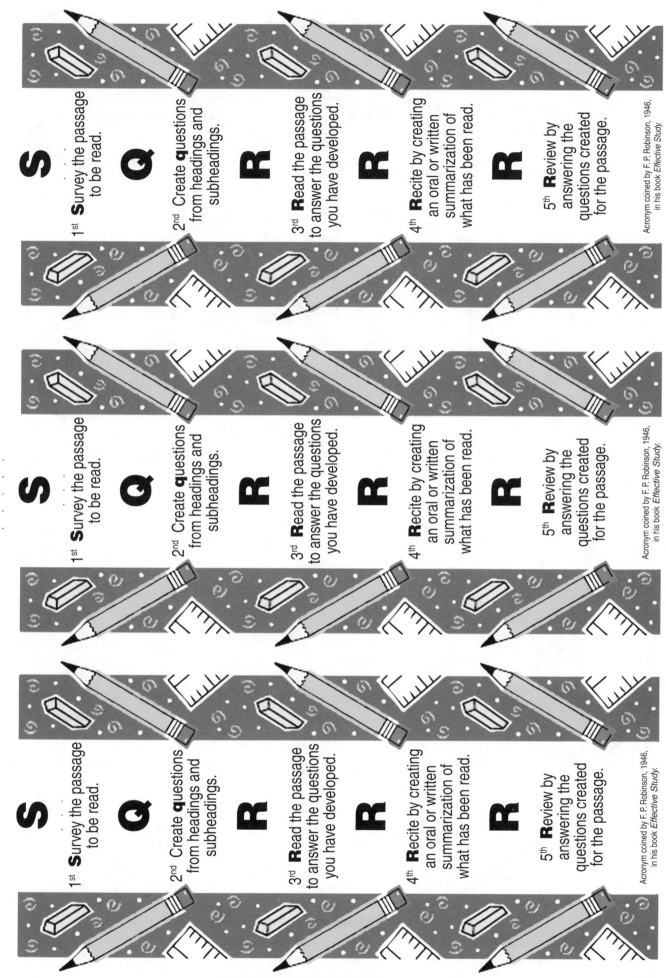

SQ3R

S

1st **Survey** the passage to be read.

Q

2nd Create **questions** from headings and subheadings.

R

3rd **Read** the passage to answer the questions you have developed.

R

4th **Recite** by creating an oral or written summarization of what has been read.

R

5th **Review** by answering the questions created for the passage.

Acronym coined by F. P. Robinson, 1946, in his book *Effective Study.*

When Was That?

THE MORE WAYS YOU TEACH, THE MORE STUDENTS YOU REACH

Gallon
(128 ounces)

Half-gallon
(64 ounces)

Quart
(32 ounces)

Pint
(16 ounces)

Cup
(8 ounces)

Cup
(8 ounces)

1. Divide ÷

2. Multiply ×

3. Subtract −

4. Check √

5. Bring down ↓

6. Remainder ↑

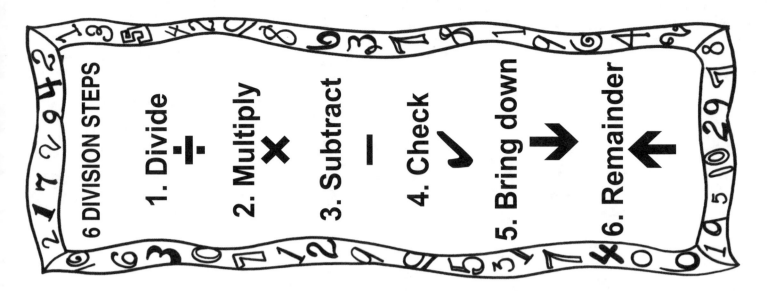

6 DIVISION STEPS

1. Divide ÷
2. Multiply ✕
3. Subtract —
4. Check ✔
5. Bring down ➡
6. Remainder ⬅

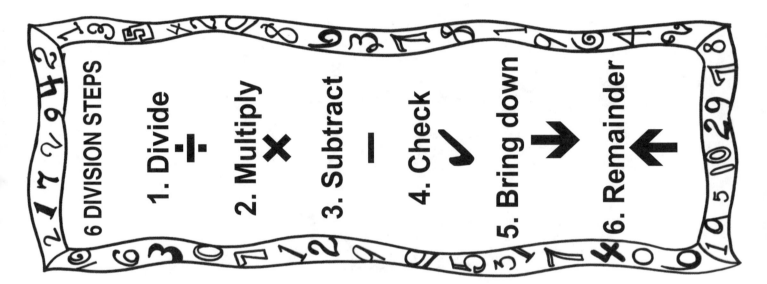

6 DIVISION STEPS

1. Divide ÷
2. Multiply ✕
3. Subtract —
4. Check ✔
5. Bring down ➡
6. Remainder ⬅

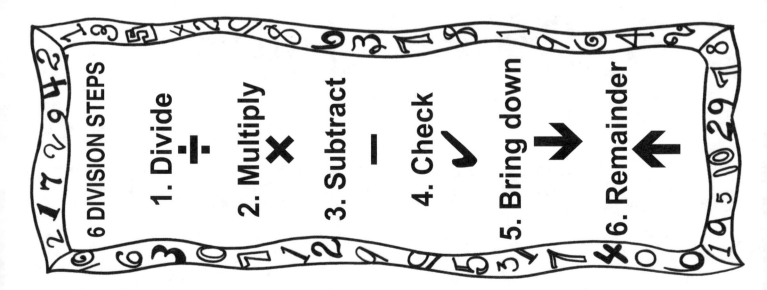

6 DIVISION STEPS

1. Divide ÷
2. Multiply ✕
3. Subtract —
4. Check ✔
5. Bring down ➡
6. Remainder ⬅

Good Luck with Your Division!

Divide ÷   Multiply ×   Subtract −   Check √   Bring down ↓   Remainder ↑

DOES McDONALD'S SELL CHEESEBURGERS RARE?

Are You Worth a Million?

A	B	C	D	E	F	G	H
1	2	3	4	5	6	7	8

I	J	K	L	M	N	O	P
9	10	11	12	13	14	15	16

Q	R	S	T	U	V	W	X
17	18	19	20	21	22	23	24

Y	Z
25	26

Example:

M   A   R   Y

$13 \times 1 \times 18 \times 25 = 5850$

(Not even close! Maybe you can do better!)

First name: _____

Numbers: _____

First and middle names: _____

Numbers: _____

First, middle, and last names: _____

Numbers: _____

Me Map Directions

1. Choose 10 events from your life that are meaningful to you. (Start with your birth.) For each event, include a time and an icon. "Time" means date, age, or school grade. "Icon" means any symbol, drawing, magazine cut-out, or computer image that represents the event. For example, the date you were born and a picture of a baby bottle might represent your birth.

2. Your events must be connected in chronological order as though you were walking a trail or following a road map. Use an emblem to connect your events and personalize your map. For example, use a series of baseballs, if you like baseball, or dog bones, if you like dogs, etc.

3. In designing your map, make it colorful, interesting, and self-explanatory. In other words, other students should have a clear overview of your life at a glance. Your map should be on a large piece of poster board.

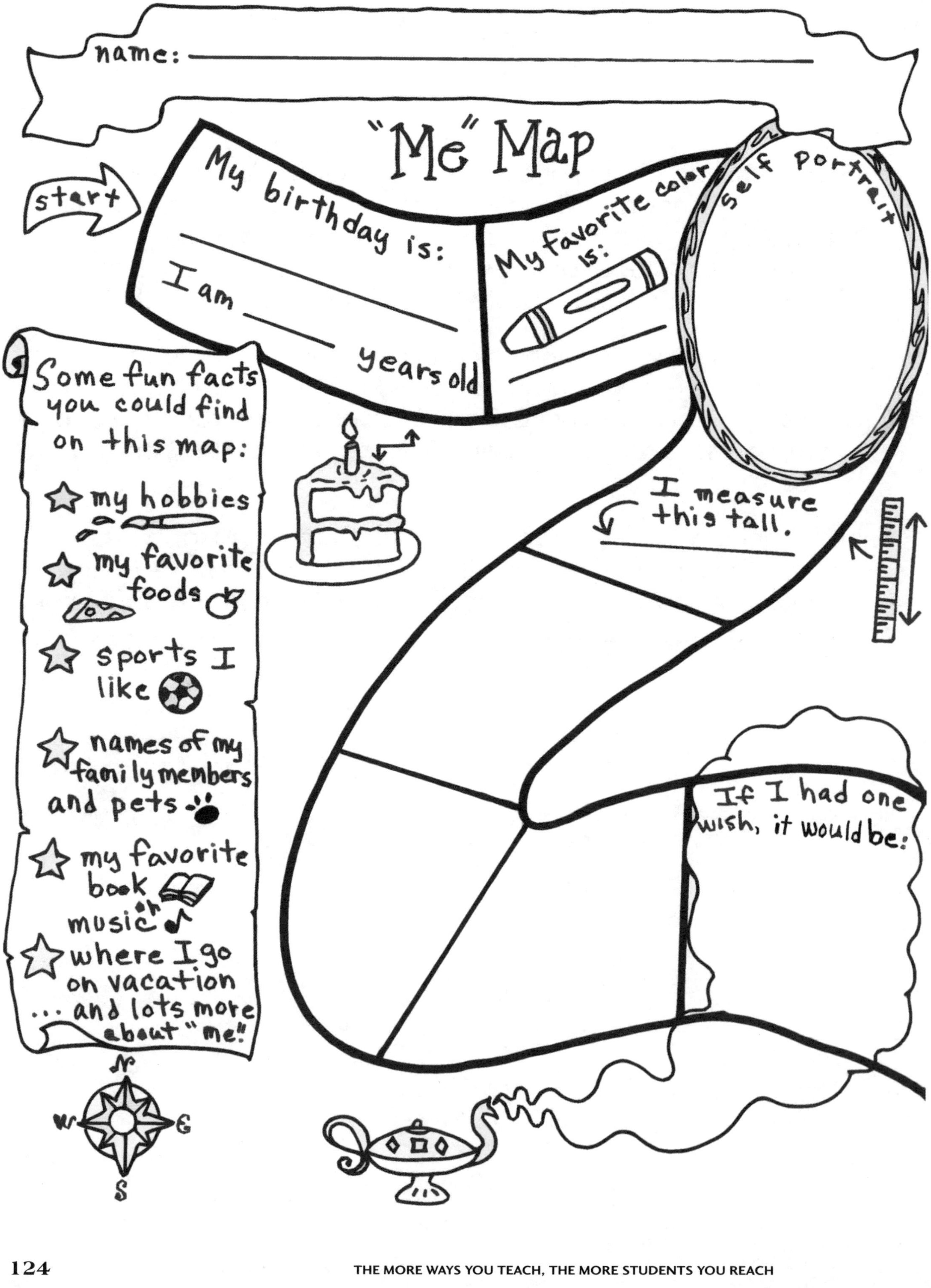

name: _____

"Me" Map

My birthday is:
_____

I am _____ years old

My favorite color is:

self portrait

Some fun facts you could find on this map:

⭐ my hobbies

⭐ my favorite foods

⭐ sports I like ⚽

⭐ names of my family members and pets

⭐ my favorite book 📖 music ♪

⭐ where I go on vacation ...and lots more about "me"!

I measure this tall.
_____

If I had one wish, it would be:

N
W   E
S

124

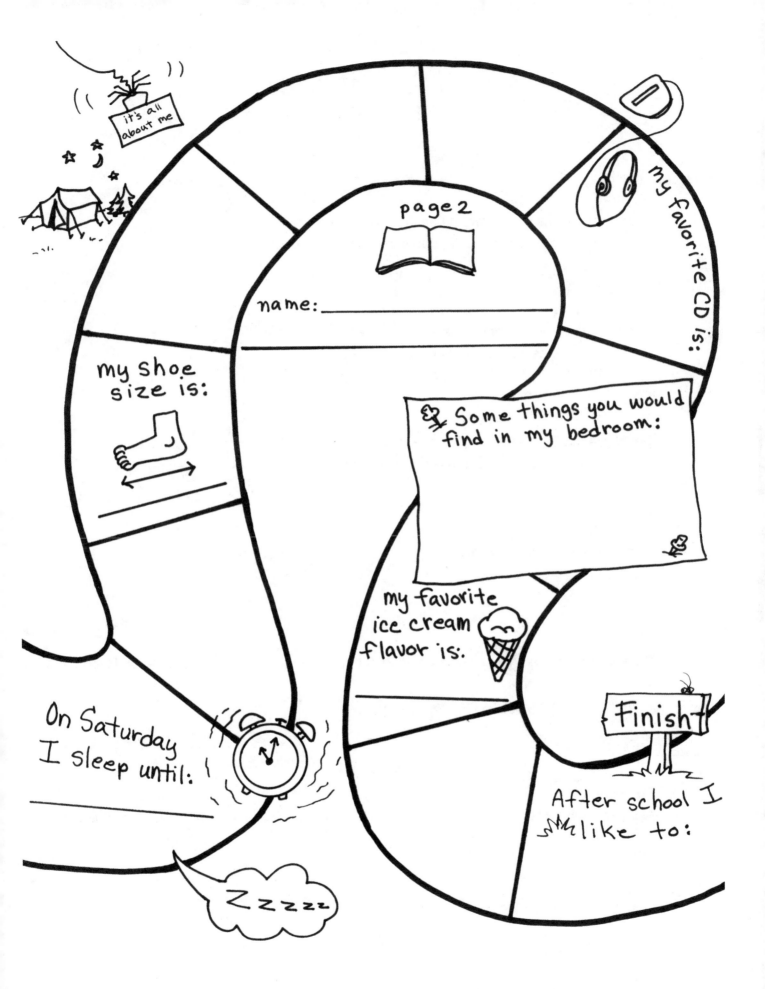

it's all about me

page 2

my favorite CD is:

my shoe size is:

name: _____

Some things you would find in my bedroom:

my favorite ice cream flavor is:

On Saturday I sleep until:
_____

Zzzzz

Finish

After school I like to:

All About Me

(Using Bloom's Taxonomy)

KNOWLEDGE

- *Define* yourself as if you were an entry in a dictionary.
- *Quote* your favorite book, movie, poem, or other passage.

COMPREHENSION

- *Paraphrase* the events of your last school year.
- *Relate* your interests to one subject area in school.

APPLICATION

- *Develop* a mission statement for this school year.
- *Relate* your interests to one subject area in school.

ANALYSIS

- *Compare* yourself to an animal.
- *Diagram* your dream house.

SYNTHESIS

- *Collaborate* with another classmate to find out three new items about one another. Record the items you learned on this paper.
- *Compile* a list of adjectives that best describe you.

EVALUATION

- *Persuade* your parents to purchase an item you currently wish to own in exactly five sentences.
- *Make* recommendations as to how this can be a successful school year for you and the class.

Story Cubes

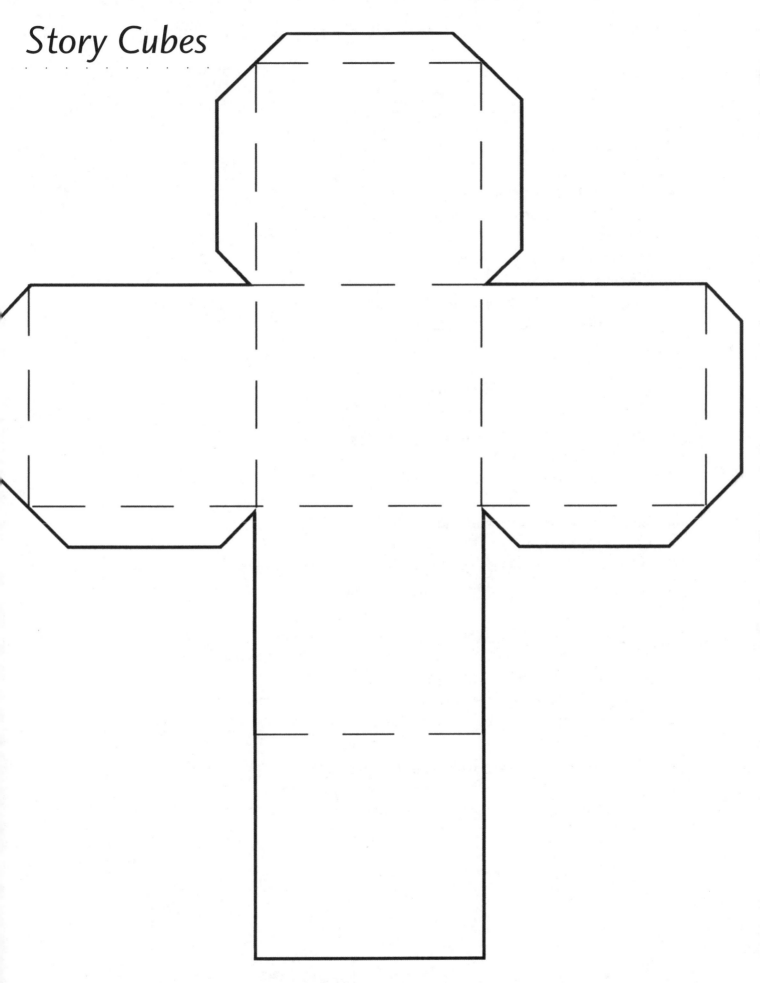

Bloom's Cube

LITERATURE

KNOWLEDGE
- Who is the main character?
- Who is the author?
- State two things that happened in the story.
- List two other books by this author.

COMPREHENSION
- List two words used to describe the main character.
- Describe the character's actions.
- State something that happened in the beginning, middle, and end of the story.
- Retell the story in your own words.
- Write a summary of the story.

APPLICATION
- Create a timeline of the events in the story.
- Write a letter to the main character.
- Illustrate the climax or turning point of the story.
- Act out a scene or event.
- Create a poster that tells about the main events.

ANALYSIS
- Compare the main character with yourself.
- What other books have you read with similar messages?
- Use a Venn Diagram to compare this author's style with the style of your favorite author.
- Compare this book to another one by the same author.

SYNTHESIS
- Add yourself to the original story and write about your role.
- Write a sequel to the book that reveals how the character matures.
- Transform the text into a reader's theater.
- Create a rap that relates the main events and end with the theme of the book.
- Create an award for this book and explain the award's significance.

EVALUATION
- Write a review of this book for your local newspaper.
- Judge the character's actions according to what you think is right or not right.
- Write a letter to the media specialist convincing her to buy or not buy this book for our school's library.

THE MORE WAYS YOU TEACH, THE MORE STUDENTS YOU REACH

Think-Tac-Toe

IMAGINE (SYNTHESIS) You are the main character in the story. How would you do things differently? **1**	**LOCATE** (KNOWLEDGE) Find the page where the author writes about the plot's turning point. **2**	**RESPOND** (COMPREHENSION) Respond to the author by writing him or her a friendly letter. **3**
COMPARE (COMPREHENSION) Compare this story with another one with the same theme. **4**	**CREATE** (SYNTHESIS) Come up with a way to share what you've read. Get your idea approved by the teacher. **5**	**BUILD** (APPLICATION) Build a diorama to show the characters and setting of the story. **6**
CHANGE (SYNTHESIS) You are the author. Change the setting and sequence of events. **7**	**DESCRIBE** (COMPREHENSION) You are a media specialist. Describe the plot and theme to a potential reader. **8**	**CRITIQUE** (EVALUATION) What is your viewpoint of the story? **9**

I have chosen to complete activities #_____, #_____, and #_____.

#5 Create: I will complete the following activity because I chose #5:

Student's Signature: _____ Date: _____

Teacher's Signature: _____ Date: _____

Assess Yourself

Name _____

Define the following words:	My Guess Date _____	Actual Meaning Date _____	How is your guess different from your final answer?
1.			
2.			
3.			
4.			
5.			
6.			
7.			
8.			
Categorize _____ 1. 2. 3.	Categorize _____ 1. 2. 3.	Categorize _____ 1. 2. 3	Make a Prediction: What will the text be about?

Thought Is Taught

Teacher Responses That Encourage Further Thinking

"That shows a lot of thought."

"You are on the right track."

"Who can add to that?"

"I appreciate your answer."

"Your response shows you are thinking."

"Any other thoughts or suggestions?"

"Your brain is in gear. Can anyone add something?"

"Let's build on that comment."

"Could you please summarize (name of student)'s point?"

"Describe how you arrived at your answer."

"There is no single answer for this question. I want you to consider alternatives."

Thinking Words Teachers Can Use

Instead of saying:	Say:
"Let's look at these two pictures."	"Let's compare these two pictures."
"What do you think will happen when…"	"What do you predict will happen…?"
"How can you put into groups…?"	"How can you classify…?"
"Let's work this problem."	"Let's analyze this problem."
"What did you think of this story?"	"What conclusions can you draw?"
"How can you explain…?"	"What hypothesis do you have that might explain…?"
"How do you know that's true?"	"What evidence do you have to support…?"
"How else could you use this…?"	"How could you apply this…?"

Differentiating with the Overactive Student in Mind

1. Give students something to do with their hands, e.g., squeeze ball, Play-Doh, clay, Wikki Stix, etc. Provide some students with a "Fidget box," filled with items that can be "fliddled" with. Place a foot-long Velcro strip on the underside of the student's desk, which can have a calming effect when rubbed. Provide a mouse pad that the student can quietly tap on when needed.

2. Attach a bungee cord around the front legs of the student's chair, about 4 inches above the floor, which makes a bouncing footrest. Provide students with a 12-inch foot roller, which can be made from a noodle flotation device.

3. Provide two desks, one on each end of the classroom, and allow students to move between the two desks as needed.

4. Provide a rocking chair, with felt glued onto the bottom of the runners. Allow students to use a large physical therapy ball as a chair.

5. Encourage thigh tapping.

6. Attach a tennis ball to the bottom of each chair leg. (Split the tennis ball with a razor blade, but be careful: Slicing a tennis ball could cause an allergic reaction to latex.)

7. Allow students to stand when they work and encourage toe rocking.

8. Provide opportunities for physical movement in the classroom.

9. Encourage students to lean against a wall or bookcase as a way to increase their feeling of security by being "grounded."

10. Allow students to hold a weighted lap pillow, or wear a weighted vest (the vest must be set up by a specialist, such as a special ed teacher, psychologist, nurse, etc.). Allow students to wear a heavy coat in class. Lay a sand-filled door-draft-stopper across their lap, which some students find therapeutic to massage.

Homework Recording Sheet

Assignment	Date Assigned	Date Due

Editing Checklist

❏ Punctuation is correct.

❏ Spelling is correct.

❏ Capitals are used correctly.

❏ Sentences are complete.

❏ Writing is within margins.

❏ Writing/typing is neat.

❏ First sentence in each paragraph is indented.

Editing Checklist

☐ Punctuation is correct.

☐ Spelling is correct.

☐ Capitals are used correctly.

☐ Sentences are complete.

☐ Writing is within margins.

☐ Writing/typing is neat.

☐ First sentence in each paragraph is indented.

Editing Checklist

☐ Punctuation is correct.

☐ Spelling is correct.

☐ Capitals are used correctly.

☐ Sentences are complete.

☐ Writing is within margins.

☐ Writing/typing is neat.

☐ First sentence in each paragraph is indented.

Editing Checklist

☐ Punctuation is correct.

☐ Spelling is correct.

☐ Capitals are used correctly.

☐ Sentences are complete.

☐ Writing is within margins.

☐ Writing/typing is neat.

☐ First sentence in each paragraph is indented.

WHO

HOW

WHAT

WHEN

WHERE

WHY

WHICH

ARE

CAN

DO

DOES

DID

WILL

HAVE

IS

HAS

SHOULD

WOULD

Capitalization Rules

Mickey Mouse	names of people
Thanksgiving Day	holidays
Empire State Building	names of buildings
Sunday	days of the week
January	months of the year
Main Street	names of streets
Dublin, New Hampshire	cities and states
North America	continents
United States	countries
Dear Fred,	letter greeting
Sincerely yours,	first word of letter closing
A Wrinkle in Time	titles (first, last, and all important words in-between)
The sun dipped slowly.	first word in a sentence
"We are here," Tim said.	first word in a quote

THE MORE WAYS YOU TEACH, THE MORE STUDENTS YOU REACH

Hundreds Chart

1	2	3	4	5	6	7	8	9	10
11	12	13	14	15	16	17	18	19	20
21	22	23	24	25	26	27	28	29	30
31	32	33	34	35	36	37	38	39	40
41	42	43	44	45	46	47	48	49	50
51	52	53	54	55	56	57	58	59	60
61	62	63	64	65	66	67	68	69	70
71	72	73	74	75	76	77	78	79	80
81	82	83	84	85	86	87	88	89	90
91	92	93	94	95	96	97	98	99	100

Graphic Artist

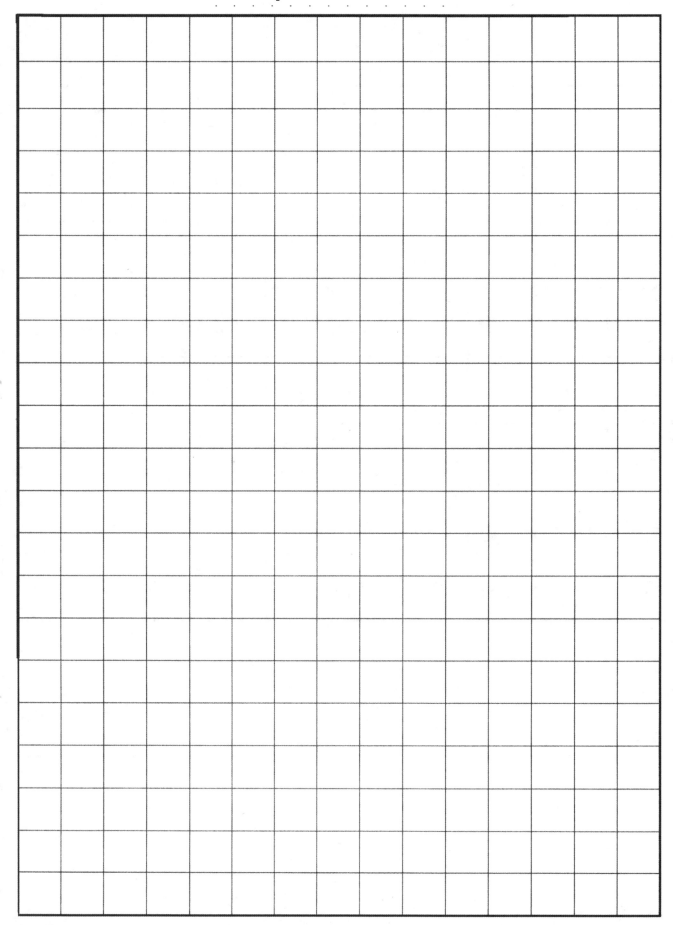

THE MORE WAYS YOU TEACH, THE MORE STUDENTS YOU REACH

Response Spinner

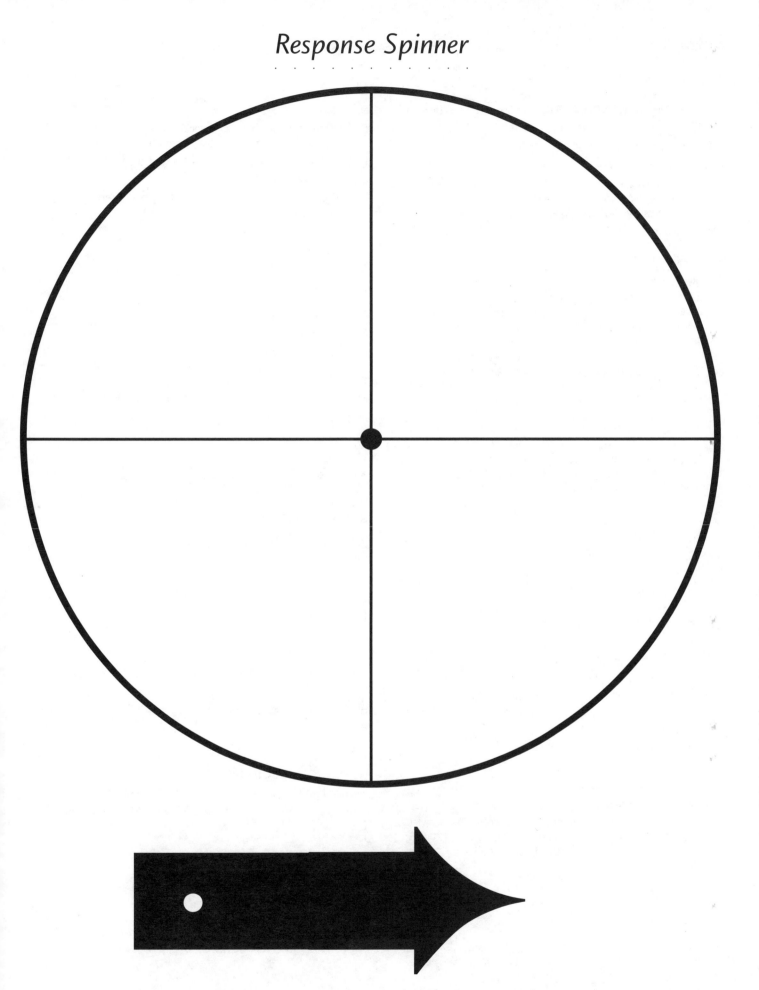

INDEX

Page numbers of Reproducibles appear in **boldface** type.

THE MORE WAYS YOU TEACH, THE MORE STUDENTS YOU REACH